CW00322128

THE <u>NEW</u> FESSTAMENT

First published in Great Britain in 2023 by Radar,
an imprint of
Octopus Publishing Group Ltd
Carmelite House
50 Victoria Embankment
London EC4Y 0DZ
www.octopusbooks.co.uk

An Hachette UK Company
www.hachette.co.uk

Distributed in the US by
Hachette Book Group
1290 Avenue of the Americas
4th and 5th Floors
New York, NY 10104

Distributed in Canada by
Canadian Manda Group
664 Annette St.
Toronto, Ontario, Canada M6S 2C8

ISBN 978-1-80419-042-5

A CIP catalogue record for this book is available from the British Library.

Printed and bound in Great Britain

1 3 5 7 9 10 8 6 4 2

All images: Internet Archive Book Images

This FSC® label means that materials used for the product have been responsibly sourced.

THE VERY BEST OF
FESS
HOLE

THE NEW FESSTAMENT

Rob Manuel

RADAR

For The Archbishop

of Canterbury,

Sir Clive Sinclair

and happy

sinners everywhere

> "Whoever conceals
> their sins does not
> prosper, but the one who
> confesses and renounces
> them finds mercy."

Proverbs 28:13

"BIG
DOG'S
COCK"

Rude Kid

Viz (1987)

INTRODUCTION

How do you follow a book that many believed was the new Bible for our culture?

Well, I thought, the Bible had the Old Testament, and then when that was a hit, God wrote the New Testament, so here it is, the *NEW FESSTAMENT*.

You asked for it. You asked for more Fesshole and you've got it. The stories keep coming in: so far we've had over two hundred thousand confessions submitted, that's eight million words. But never mind the quantity, feel the quality – this is just the very best.

* * *

When people ask me how Fesshole started, I tell different stories. They're all true, but which one I tell depends on the moment. So take your pick from the following options:

1.   I like funny stories.

2.   I was bored one afternoon and thought people typing confessions into a Google form and tweeting a few out would be good fun.

3.   I wanted a hit Twitter account because I was working on a project where an 'influencer' was being paid a silly amount of money. I asked the ad agency, 'How can I get paid this kind of money?' They said, 'Well, they've got a million followers. You don't.' Right, I could have a

go. When Fesshole did start hitting those numbers, I went back and they said, 'Not like that, Rob. Adidas don't want to promo their new trainers against 4,000 stories about wanking.'

4. I was running a silly Twitter account called Swear Clock that tweeted out the time – 'Sorry I'm late, I shat myself in Lidl, it's 7am' – and I asked for user suggestions. This produced a funny document and I thought, "Hmmm, people seem to like this, I should do it again about another subject."

5. I was running another Twitter account for Anonymous Opinions and my friend Chris – the designer of this very book – said he liked it and that I should do more with it.

6. I used to run a funny stories section on the website B3ta.com (Question of the Week) and it had ground to a halt because, quite frankly, most people have gravitated off forums and onto social media. The most basic rule of entertainment is go to where the people are, so I thought I'd do something similar on Twitter and found it worked even better there because the character limit made all the stories short and easy to read.

7. Maybe the whole thing exists because my gut bacteria needed to make sure money was coming so that there was delicious food in my stomach for the microbes to feast on.

All these things are true and the lesson here is there's rarely a single origin story for anything. Maybe there's even another: Fesshole exists because our collective consciousness needs a route to let out a howl of humour and pain. I'm not its creator, more a midwife who birthed it into the world.

Anyway. Enjoy the confessions. I have suffered to bring them to you – no one else in the world is reading 200 to 400 confessions every day of his life to supply you with the very best stories mankind has to offer.

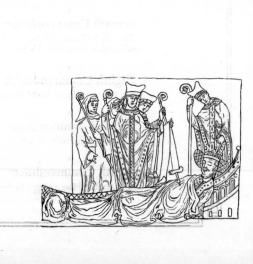

The <u>NEW</u> Fesshole Ten Commandments

x

First Commandment
Thou Shalt Honour and Love Your Partner

x

Second Commandment
Thou Shalt Use These Shonky Tips

x

Third Commandment
Thou Shalt Parent Like a Parenting Bastard

x

Fourth Commandment
Thou Shalt Have a Brain Completely Consumed By Sex

x

Fifth Commandment
Thou Shalt Have Largely Negative Feelings About Work

x

Sixth Commandment
Thou Shalt Love Your Home-life (and House)

x

Seventh Commandment
Thou Shalt Obtain Self-Awareness
and Laugh at Thine Own Uselessness

x

Eighth Commandment
Thou Shalt Perceive a Bigger World Than Thyself

x

Ninth Commandment
Thou Shalt Eventually Die

x

Tenth Commandment
But Thou Shalt Have a Happy Ending

x

Thou Shalt Honour and Love Your Partner

Relationships are tricky.

On the one hand

they are the source of everything

that is good in the world,

on the other hand, familiarity breeds

unwashed socks and weight gain.

My partner and I did the 'hall pass' thing where you get to choose one person you can sleep with consequence-free. She chose Ryan Reynolds. I chose Lisa from work. Haven't been allowed to a work function since.

My friends have truly beautiful wedding photos all round their homes. I have none as I wore a trouser suit to a registry office and in the only picture taken, my husband and I look like *Bullseye* contestants from the Jim Bowen era.

When my wife wants my assistance in another part of the house, she just yells my name. I refuse to move unless she actually says, 'Can you come here please', which she never does, so we're just stuck in a rut of her bellowing my name & me screaming back 'WHAT?' It's pretty grim.

Failed Romantic Gestures

Cupid's arrow rarely flies straight as we're all such terrible shots.

On a date with a girl I was besotted with, tried to show off my 'bad boy' side by taking her to my dealer's after closing time for a bag. I ended up lying awake on his couch listening to him shag her all night.

In the early days of smart phones, a girl asked me to send her a picture of my cock. I was a bit bemused but obliged. She messaged back, 'OK – but I meant with a hard-on.'

I've been considering popping the question. My son had a packet of Love Hearts and the top one was 'Marry Me'. On the spur of the moment I told him to give it to Mummy and say it's from Daddy. She said, 'Ah, that's nice,' and ate it. That was literally my proposal. Never again.

Dating

The trick to getting a date is be like our friend Paul, who in the days of MySpace wrote code to send a message to every woman in a 10-mile radius saying 'Hey' and anyone who replied, well, they were a prospect, the lucky ladies.

Been married 18 years, thought I'd try my chances on Tinder. Turns out I'm as attractive as dog shit on your shoe on a hot day. Bought the wife some flowers. Thank god I'm not single.

In my late 20s I was seeing seven different guys; they each had their own night. It all ended when I had to see *Iron Man 3* five times in a week.

The wife loves Michael Bublé.
When we first started dating I told
her I did too in order impress her.
Must have spent about £2k
seeing him live over the years.
Can't stand him.

6

I've had a number of affairs with women I met through Tinder. When I want to get rid of them, I don't tell them that my feelings have changed, I just say that I've had to take a lower-paying job and am now skint. They just disappear. Works every time.

Once asked a pretty but not-very-bright girl out on a date. She – genuinely – misunderstood and arranged a date... only for her brother to turn up. Turned out she thought I was gay. And thought he was gay. Neither of us were.

I used to drive a JCB digger. One night I took a girl back to my flat and next morning offered her a lift home. She duly accepted, I went outside and jumped in the digger. Fair play to her, she climbed up into the cab and I dropped her off outside the bank.

I recently signed up to a site for married people looking for affairs. I'm single but it works so much better than dating apps and if I can't be arsed to see them again or to meet because I'm watching football, I blame my imaginary wife. Why didn't I discover this sooner?

When I broke up with my ex, she left moisturiser in my flat. Naturally I thought, 'Good for wanking.' Didn't realise it was gradual tanning moisturiser. Now my dick is a completely different ethnicity from the rest of me and I can't start dating as a result. Think she planned it.

How We Met

If you're a Hollywood scriptwriter, here are your ideas for 'meet-cutes' for your next rom-com.

Met a girl in a club. Went back to hers, both hammered. Woke up with a Staffie in bed with us. So I went downstairs, let him out in the garden and threw a ball for him. Girl was so impressed she cooked me breakfast. Three years on, me, girl and dog still together.

FAV: 28,465 RT: 287

Went on a date five years ago. It was shit so sat in the toilet playing with my phone for 30 mins. Came out and told her I was ill and needed to go home, she insisted on coming with me. She took such good care I fell in love. I'd hate her to find out I found her boring.

FAV: 9,317 RT: 99

My partner of 15 years will never know that our first date only happened as stage two of a succesful mission to sleep with three people who shared the same first name in the space of one weekend.

FAV: 3,377 RT: 48

In 2002 I drove my Ford Sierra into a lamppost. Nobody was hurt, except my pride. The woman who ran over to see if I was OK ended up marrying me. She'll never know I crashed because I was busy staring at her fantastic arse.

FAV: 8,744 RT: 117

I met my now wife at a swingers party we both reluctantly went to with partners and hated it. We ended up talking all night and swapped numbers. We tell people we met on eHarmony. I saw her tits before speaking to her and she saw what I was packing and still went out with me.

When first seeing a girl, she quite enjoyed a finger in the arse during foreplay. One time a small pebble of poo came out. At the end, too embarrassed to get rid of it, I put it back in her. We are now married and to this day have never spoken about it or performed the act again.

Husband Hacks

Does your husband need to be kicked into line? Try sulking at him or refusing sex.

My husband likes taking mucky photos of me in the nude. I don't mind, mainly because I've realised that he always does a brilliant job of tidying the bedroom up before we do it. I've started suggesting different rooms round the house; the en-suite needs a good scrub.

I give my husband a £30 gift voucher every year for his birthday. He always leaves it hanging around, under piles of rubbish or in a messy drawer. I take it and give it back to him next year. I haven't bought him a gift since 2016.

The kids think their dad is on their chores reward chart to show that 'everyone in the house does their bit' etc – actually it's so Dad can see how close Mum is to allowing him to do it up the bum at the weekend. House has never been cleaner.

When my WFH days line up with my husband's, I put on my magic leggings and do as much gratuitous bending over near him as I can. He's going to jump me eventually and I'd rather get it out the way early. Few quick pumps and I can work in peace for the rest of the day.

My husband's drinking started really annoying me, so I added yellow food dye to his shower gel. A week later he gave up drinking and went on a health kick.

Wife Hacks

How to have an excellent time at home by training your wife with absolute bullshit that in no way will ever bite you in the arse.

I wanted my partner to get me a mystery football shirt box for my birthday, so about a month before I googled a load of them from her phone so they'd come up on her targeted ads. It worked.

My wife had to sign a non-disclosure agreement, so she can't talk to me about her work. This is great because it's really boring.

I will instigate sex in the morning with my wife, knowing that she will rebuff my advances and instantly get up and make me coffee in bed.

Whenever I want to buy myself a new sex toy without my wife knowing, I buy it just before HER birthday, or Christmas. The unmarked box arrives in the post, and I can take it away and say, 'Ooh! A gift for SOMEONE!' Me. It's a gift for me. And my prostate.

I bought an identical thermostat for the heating. Hid the real one & set it to 18°C and left the false one in the usual place so my wife can turn it up to 25°C + with no effect .

When we first got married, I told my wife that I had an unusual fetish and doing the washing up made me extremely horny – something to do with rubber gloves and hot soapy water. After a few weeks, my wife got fed up with this and banned me from ever doing the washing up again.

I Lie to My Man

White lies in a relationship keep things fresh. No one needs to know about the massive log you just did that was the size of a Bismark destoyer. Shut up, Camilla.

I am meant to be on a diet as my husband says he would love me more if I was slimmer. I secretly eat Flakes in bed and brush the crumbs onto his side. The resulting 'skid marks' have led the shallow judgemental bastard to believe his personal hygiene is somewhat lacking.

FAV: 10,282 RT: 129

At Tesco the other week I asked my BF to check the notes in my phone for a shopping list I had written. He found a long list of names and asked me what it was. I told him it was a list of potential baby names I like, but it's actually everyone I've ever shagged.

FAV: 5,965 RT: 90

My boyfriend has a mild nut allergy, itchy hives, not lethal. When he pisses me off I eat a Snickers bar in my sluttiest underwear.

FAV: 11,500 RT: 204

When my husband texts me jokes, I have learned not to bother reading them anymore, I just reply with '😀😀😀' because the jokes are always shit.

FAV: 5,304 RT: 68

**When I take my little boy to the park I feel the
need to repeatedly call his name while he plays
so the other parents don't think I'm just a paedo
on a bench.**

My southern husband is very sniffy about 'northern'
water and insists on buying posh bottled water from
Waitrose. Little does he know this is what gets poured
into the dog's water bowl and his bottle gets filled up
with dirty northern muck.

I Lie to My Woman

Men who say they don't lie to their women are liars.

**My girlfriend is out of my league. A pretty, kind and
very intelligent brunette who blokes stare at when
we're out. But sometimes, I can't be bothered with
her so I tell her I'm visiting family in Kent, then I have
a weekend watching tank videos on YouTube.**

About a year ago, the company I worked for switched to
a four-day week. Never told my wife. Each Friday, I hire
out a small office where I play *Football Manager*. I like to
pretend its my manager's office. I have 'conversations'
with players about disciplinary matters and contracts.

I have a secret non-stick frying pan which I hide from my wife and kids. I use it to fry the perfect sunny-side-up eggs etc. I use it when everyone is out. My family kept scratching MY other pans and ruined them. Had it one year and it's as good as the day I bought it.

My wife asked me why I was distant and anxious, I told her there was a work issue with a colleague. In reality I was struggling to sign a quality right back on *Championship Manager*.

Once after sex my wife broke down in tears asking if I was cheating on her because I didn't finish. I reassured her it was just because I was tired when in reality I had already had three wanks that day and wasn't expecting sex that night.

Helped my wife start up an OnlyFans account last year, but also set up my own secret account which I use to send her requests, which I then help her film and sometimes star in. Cost me hundreds but I get to have porn-style sex while she gets a boost from having fans.

My partner of four years still thinks our meeting was 'fate' when actually it was the most planned-out one night stand attempt I've ever tried, which included re-arranging work, buying tickets to a show I didn't like and perfectly timing 'bumping into' them. Worked perfectly.

The biggest secret I keep in
our house is that I have a secret
wormery in the garden.
My partner kept saying
I couldn't have a wormery,
so now I sneak out to feed
them scraps when she's at work.
Love my secret worms.

I Cheated On Her

Do you know how most cheats get caught? They tell people.
Keep schtum, you morons.

Wife gleefully showed me footage of two people
making out in the alley next to our house. Grateful
for rubbish CCTV, it was me and her best friend.
Forgot about the cameras.

FAV: 12,443 RT: 219

I hired a cleaner who turned out to be useless and
misses whole rooms but I won't get rid of her because
her hair is exactly the same as the woman from work
I'm having an affair with and that accounts for any 'stray
hairs' at home.

FAV: 4,051 RT: 61

Was seriously romantically involved with another
woman for a few years and my wife found out. They
talked on the telephone and, surprisingly, got along
and became friends. Now they're in a book club
together and text every day – meanwhile I've never
felt more lonesome.

FAV: 6,381 RT: 69

Having an affair makes me better. Got married in 2018,
life became boring, started having an affair with wife's
friend. I got a new job, lost weight, went out more. Affair
ended when she got married, now having another affair
with someone else. Same thing happened.

FAV: 3,232 RT: 45

I Cheated On Him

If you're going to cheat on your man, do it quietly. Most men just don't want the humiliation.

My passwords are all the names of people I've had sex with since being married. I'm really hoping my husband doesn't want to log into my Spotify account.

My son has brown eyes. My husband and I both have blue. Genetically, it's impossible that he's his father, but he's not very good at biology, so he doesn't know. I dread the day he learns this piece of trivia. Luckily, he looks like him because he's actually his nephew.

I've been dating this guy for 3 months and he forgot my birthday, so I had a one night stand. The guy hadn't forgotten, he'd planned a surprise party. I feel terrible and he still doesn't know.

I cheat on my husband with a man with the same name, so I never have to worry about getting his name wrong.

I left my husband for another man, and he left his wife for me. We had great sex to begin with – one of the main reasons why I fell for him – but now that the novelty of sneaking around and cheating has worn off, it's like being married. Now I have to fake my orgasms again.

I Am Irritated With Her

If men weren't moaning about 'er indoors, then is it really a heterosexual marriage at all?

My wife has the loudest voice ever. It's like living with Brian Blessed. Everyone comments and kids cringe in public. I'm monitoring how loud she is via a dB app. She's averaging 80dB for normal conversation. It's excruciating. Told her and she doesn't give a shit. She's 9st and 5ft 1.

My wife thinks it's adorable and kooky that she loses her keys daily. In reality, it's a big part of why I'm going to divorce her. THERE IS A SET OF HOOKS FOR KEYS BEHIND THE DOOR, HANG YOUR KEYS ON THERE, YOU LITERALLY BOUGHT THE HOOKS.

I love my wife. But there is one thing I can't stand. When we go out for food and she says she doesn't want pudding and then she always asks for a second spoon when mine arrives. After 18 years it still does my nut in.

My wife passive-aggressively
points out my failings to the dog
when I'm in earshot. I tell her this
is pathetic, but when she goes out,
I sit him down and give him my
account of events at length.

I've been keeping tabs for a few months. It takes an average of one hour and 42 minutes to watch one hour of TV with my wife.

> My wife adds .com every time she says the word 'confused'. It's one of my pet hates and I have to live with it.
>

My girlfriend thinks she's hilarious but has the worst comedic timing I've ever experienced. To top it off, she blurts out her one-liners too quick and then shouts 'waheey' like a teenager. Every time I force out a laugh I die a little more inside, but I absolutely adore her.

I Am Getting the Ick About Him

Once you've got the ick, it's all downhill. Dump them, girlfriend. Or go for a walk.

My boyfriend has a personalised registration plate and it makes me cringe so hard, I'm embarrassed to drive where people might know me.

My boyfriend is called Matthew. A few months ago I called his penis 'Little Matthew' when I was drunk. He thought it was cute and now refers to it as Little Matthew all the time, saying things like 'Little Matthew wants a kiss.' It is a massive turn-off and it's all my own fault.

Today, after I had cooked us a delicious sausage casserole, my doting boyfriend helpfully took our empty plates to the kitchen and put them in the sink, so that later I could remove them from the sink and wash them. I don't know what I would do without him.

FAV: 9,736 RT: 125

My husband voted Tory. Nothing else in 16 years has made me consider divorce more seriously.

FAV: 16,293 RT: 342

I Think My Man Is Actually Stupid

Is your man thick as two short planks? Don't worry, as long as he can wear a suit, the patriarchy means he's qualified to be at least Prime Minister.

This is a confession on behalf of my daft twat of an ex-husband who tried to iron a shirt while he was wearing it, with predictable results.

FAV: 5,482 RT: 94

More his fess than mine, but I had an ex-boyfriend who actually thought the tide times were controlled by the local council. We lived by the sea. I never told him the truth and it still makes me laugh imagining some poor council worker pressing a button to make the tide come in.

FAV: 6,939 RT: 131

My boyfriend is sweet and tender but his intelligence makes me question the relationship after he said, 'I love how your hair grows at different speeds.' I have a fringe.

Been married to my husband for 25 years. Comfortable home, three smashing kids and he's great in the bedroom. But tonight he said he's been using the crumb tray from the toaster to make breadcrumbs – that he uses in our cooking – and I think this may be our last Christmas.

My husband opened a new carton of milk when there was still some left in the old one. I asked why and he said there wasn't enough in the old one for a full glass, and he didn't want to mix the milk of two different cows. My husband is 47.

My ex-husband genuinely believed that blood circulates up one arm and down the other. I'm a doctor and I found this degree of ignorance in an adult incomprehensible, and the seeds of doubt were sown. The marriage lasted 4 months.

Just Talk to Them!

If you're in a relationship you need strong lines of communcation to keep things healthy – like these people.

I have a kink where I like people to shit on my feet. I asked my girlfriend if she wanted to try it. I am now single.

FAV: 4,411 RT: 78

Read a tweet that simply said 'Call your mum and tell her you love her.' Thought I'd give it a go. Dad called me back 10 minutes after I got off the phone and said, 'Mum's crying. She thinks you're dying and won't tell her.' Thanks, Twitter.

FAV: 30,113 RT: 922

I developed a quite strong desire for cock in my 40s. Guided by similar comments you get here – 'Just talk to her' – decided to discuss it with my wife. She hasn't shagged me since, and that was years ago. Thanks, everyone.

FAV: 5,219 RT: 45

Mild Revenge on Husband

It's all fun and games to torment your husband until he loses an eye and then you've got a one-eyed husband.

When my husband pisses me off I throw out a single one of his socks without him knowing.

FAV: 3,940 RT: 68

Husband stays up later than me some nights. Can always tell when he's wanking as his belt buckle rattles. Made a game where I try to guess when he's about to cum and send an 'I love you' WhatsApp.

When our daughter was little she'd try to get my husband's attention by calling him by his first name. It often came out as fatprick instead of Patrick. I rarely corrected her.

Been giving my husband the silent treatment for six days because he upset me and refused to say sorry as he didn't know what he had done. Remembered two days ago it was on a TV show I half watched while falling asleep. I'm too invested in the argument now to admit that, though.

Whenever my husband leaves his book in the bathroom I move his bookmark back three pages. I've been doing it for fifteen years.

Big oak tree in our garden sheds thousands of acorns, hubby is constantly clearing them and hates them. I have a supply in a bag and if he is being a dick, I throw them hard, at his head, from the bedroom window, when he is under it clearing them. I hear him cussing when one hits.

When things like my period, waxing schedule and libido line up, I decide I'll have sex with my husband that night/when he gets home etc, but sometimes he'll be an arsehole and I change my mind. If only he knew the consequences of his actions.

FAV: 3,082 RT: 17

Daughter regularly gets head lice. We all get them, bar hubby. It drives me nuts that I have to do all the treatments, so I experimented on him by putting four live ones into his hair while he slept. Still didn't take.

FAV: 3,754 RT: 32

Mild Revenge on Wife

What is even the point of having a partner if you can't mildly wind them up?

Whenever I owe money to my partner I wait until she's getting undressed and stick banknotes in her underwear suggesting she buys herself something pretty. She hates this.

FAV: 4,544 RT: 60

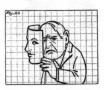

When I'm getting undressed near my wife, while the clothes are over my head I pull funny faces at her. She doesn't have a clue.

FAV: 3,121 RT: 61

I have ruined my girlfriend's love of *The Mandalorian*, as every time someone says 'This is the way' I always follow it with 'we brush our teeth'.

During nice texts with my wife she messaged, 'Your adorable'. The pedant in me managed to wait two whole minutes before replying, 'It's you're, not your – but thanks.' Caused a massive row and I would do it again.

FAV: 6,475 RT: 148

I purposely pronounce shop names wrong to annoy my girlfriend. I call Pets at Home 'Pets Come Home' and Burger King 'Burger Queen'. I've been doing it for three years and I laugh every time. She'll leave me soon.

FAV: 4,111 RT: 68

Revenge on Boyfriend

Does your boyfiend piss you off? Yeah, well, he'll be worse when he's your husband.

> **I sometimes wake my boyfriend up in the night to tell him to stop snoring. He doesn't snore, though, I just think it's funny.**
>
> FAV: 8,957 RT: 187

My boyfriend is a quick and often selfish lover. After asking him to at least touch me and make me come, he replied 'Do it yourself' and placed my hand by my vagina. I felt so rejected that I went and had sex with someone else.

FAV: 9,716 RT: 86

I found my boyfriend's wank bank. It was mostly screenshots of women's Instagrams that he knows personally. I muted all of them on his account.

Revenge on the Ex

The right thing to do with an ex is think of them, say, once a year and maybe send a Christmas card to let them know everything is cool. That's not what these people think – they're the 'sew prawns into the curtains' brigade and we're all for it.

My boyfriend broke up with me after my dad's funeral and moved out, leaving a load of books he picked up later. Ripped out the final page of each one – happy reading, dickhead.

Got a new girlfriend at the start of December, had to go round her ex's and pick up some of her stuff, he had agreed to be out. Out of our pettiness I opened the 24th door on his *Star Wars* chocolate advent calendar, scoffed the Millennium Falcon and carefully closed the door.

My ex wanted two valuable art prints in the divorce, so before I had to hand them over I took them out of the frame, had them copied and put the copies back in the frames. It's been 15 years and she has never figured it out.

Recently split with partner. We had a new car on order, paid for from his business. I've since logged in and changed the colour to a green car instead of blue. He's going to be fuming when he collects it, he's a Rangers supporter.

FAV: 9,364 RT: 212

Got cheated on by my ex after ten years together. He has a massive vinyl collection. I scratched 'cunt' into various ones in no particular order and imagine him years later picking out a particular one to play as it's been a while, but can't because it's ruined.

FAV: 4,642 RT: 43

I drive a grit lorry and everytime I get to the first tight corner just past my ex's house I turn the gritter off in hope that in the morning they'll crash.

FAV: 4,578 RT: 68

Short Doomed Relationships

One night stands are the best. You get a shag and you get to experience the full madness of another person in three dimensions. Everyone should be allowed this experience once a year as a magick rite to remind you you're alive.

I once went on a date to a girl's house. She made salad and I watched her throw away the lettuce leaves and chop up the tough stalky bits to put in the bowl. Shagged her because she was hot, but then changed my number immediately, because she was clearly also absolutely insane.

FAV: 2,995 RT: 32

A guy was supposed to drive and meet me for a date this weekend. I've known him for a while and have met him in person before. I had a look through who he follows on Twitter to see if we have any mutuals and found 80 per cent of them to be OnlyFans preview accounts. I cancelled immediately.

FAV: 3,087 RT: 38

Met a girl on a night out. Both got really drunk and ended up on going for it on the beach. Swapped numbers but I gave her a fake one. Bout a month later I realised I was her postman. No eye contact since.

FAV: 3,766 RT: 55

I really fancied this guy in a nightclub, went home with him, he walked into the house, slipped his shoes off and put some clogs on. Clogs! Wooden and all. Complete turn-off. Went home.

FAV: 4,680 RT: 66

Slightly Less Mild Revenge on Husband

Are you annoyed with your husband? Here are some handy tips to make his life miserable. You could could also advertise his job on LinkedIn just to make him paranoid.

When I was hiring a cleaner, I deliberately picked a pretty one in the hopes my husband would cheat with her and give me official grounds for a divorce. I don't think 'because I've gone off him' will cut it legally. So far, he hasn't.

FAV: 7,902 RT: 107

I've been messaging my husband from different fake accounts, sending him abuse. He's convinced he's being targeted by a hacker group. In reality he hasn't done the dishes in the three years we've been married.

FAV: 5,050 RT: 112

My husband insists on wearing his Apple Watch when having sex to track his calories burned. I wouldn't mind if he actually moved and lasted longer than 5 minutes. He'd have much better results if he gave it to his mate Gary when he's away with the army on weekends.

FAV: 15,464 RT: 319

Convinced my husband to have a vasectomy. One day after the procedure I served divorce papers and told him I knew of his ongoing nine-month-long affair with my supposed best friend. She has always wanted children.

FAV:22,155 RT:618

Why I Dumped Her

It's OK to dump people. Sometimes they just need to go into the recycling bin along with the banana peel and Shakin' Stevens records.

Got divorced because of a multipack of Twirls. Wife had her two and then demanded one of mine. I refused as she was being greedy and it escalated from there. Admittedly we had other issues going on but that was the final straw.

FAV: 20,531 RT: 403

My amazing wife took me away for
my 40th birthday, the holiday
house was amazing and I was
looking forward to some peace and
relaxing. I walked into the next room
and my entire family was there.
Instead of being delighted,
I very audibly said, 'For fuck's sake.'

I dated a girl who would put the milk in first when making a cuppa and I thought this psychotic behaviour. Several years on, I've found out she's been arrested for smashing up her new BF's car because he stayed out after his curfew. Trust your instincts.

I once dated a girl who had a Santa Claus fetish. She wanted to be spanked by Santa for being on his naughty list etc. She even wanted me to wear a Santa hat while doing it. Did it. Never again. Had to dump her. Still get weirded out walking past Santa's grottos every Xmas.

I've moved in with my girlfriend of four months. She has a box of her childhood teeth. Well, she says they're hers but there are five canines in there. Time to leave.

I own 1000s of CDs and vinyl records. When dating years ago I was told 'When we are living together, those will have to go.' I just laughed, but in my head I was thinking, 'No, you'll be gone before they are.' We broke up two months later, never told her why. I'm still alone.

Went on couples hols with four couples. I was pudgy compared to my mates. Overheard my wife say to the other wives, 'Here's the Chippendales & their chubby minder.' Pretended not to hear. Revenge was getting in serious shape, sleeping with her sis and dumping her. The comment still hurts.

Why I Dumped Him

If you're on the fence about whether to get out, maybe these people can help find your inspiration to end up listlessly looking at dating apps going, 'But they're all awful.'

I've just dumped my boyfriend after discovering he doesn't put salt on his food or in his cooking – and not for health reasons. What kind of psycho can eat chips with no salt?

My husband told me he could 'give me' everything: 'kitchens, ski holidays'. What he actually gave me was an STD from a prostitute. Now I'm 'giving him' a divorce.

I once told my boyfriend I didn't want sex because it was the time of the month. He drunkenly came up with the rhyme, 'Please babe don't be a quitter, let me do you up the shitter.' I dumped him as soon as he sobered up.

Romance Is Not Dead

These people truly understand that you keep the relationship alive through mystery.

Sometimes I have sex with my husband so I don't have to be bored while I wait for my phone to charge.

My girlfriend often asks what my favourite-ever date of ours is. I say one of our first, a romantic walk in the park when it was snowing. But really, it was when we were drunk and she let me put it up her arse.

FAV: 13,020 RT: 276

Me and my girlfriend like to sniff each other's farts. We have a monthly competition where the person who does the worst fart that month buys the other takeout.

FAV: 3,272 RT: 55

I thought having an en suite would be cool but my wife takes a shit every night, rather than in the morning like normal people, and the reek stays in our bedroom and keeps me awake. It's unholy and foul, like a sick dog has shat out its bowels.

FAV: 13,268 RT: 282

I Love Her

No jokes, these people just love their woman.

My girlfriend works in a restaurant and when any of her colleagues are unnecessarily mean to her I write a bad review, mention the colleague by name and make up something bad about their service.

FAV: 3,732 RT: 22

My wife is easily a 9 out of 10. I'm a 3 at best. I'm not rich or good in the sack. Spend all my waking life waiting for her to to realise what she could have. Keep wondering if it's all a reality TV wind-up.

FAV: 13,383 RT: 208

At any moment, either my girlfriend or I can declare 'tummy time', at which point we both lift our tops and slowly rub our tummies together. We can't remember who first suggested it but we like the sensation and have been doing it since the day we met.

My mates all think that my wife doesn't let me go to the pub anymore. In reality, I would much rather spend the evening with her and the kids and then cuddle up with a glass of wine and a film than listen to drunken twats talk bollocks about football.

I used to work on the production line of a sweet factory and my wife would love me coming home smelling of sweets. But since my promotion I work in the office, so when I finish I hang around near the production line for 30 minutes so that when I get home I still smell nice for my wife.

After a few bottles of wine my wife took off her knickers, put them on my head and crowned me 'queen of the house'. I then took off my boxers and crowned her 'king of the house'. It took a couple of hours before we realised our living room curtains were open.

I Love Him

No gags – these people just love their man and want you to know.

When I met my now fiancé he told me he didn't like animals much. He seemed otherwise great so I chose not to believe him. Eight years on he gleefully phoned me at work to tell me our cat has the zoomies again. Mission accomplished.

FAV: 7,731 RT: 69

This Christmas we both told our parents that we were with the other one's family. Actually spent the day at home with each other, curled up on the sofa watching *Lord of the Rings* in our pyjamas and eating roast potatoes dipped in gravy. It was perfect.

FAV: 44,215 RT: 663

I leave for work before hubby gets up and he ALWAYS sleepily reaches out for my hand as I leave – every day for the last ten years – and I haven't told him it's one of my favourite parts of the day, because he might overthink it and stop doing it.

FAV: 28,713 RT: 420

My wife and I don't have a 'side' in our bed. Whoever goes to bed just picks a side and that's theirs for the night. Not sure I can tell any friends or family as they'd probably think we're murderers.

FAV:26,628 RT:767

HAVE YOUR SAY

~~~~~~

We couldn't publish this book without some of our favourite comments from the readers. It is, after all, YOU who make Fesshole what it is... you filthy, disgusting perverts.

My husband has started whispering 'Time for tubby custard' just before he orgasms. I don't know how much longer I can stay with him.

Hi Carrie, as he's no longer Prime Minister, I'd suggest you get out as quick as you can.

My wife was heavily pregnant so I had one last night out with the boys, went back to this girl's place, had the best sex I've ever had in my life. That same woman delivered my child three weeks later. Not a word said between us. I wanted to die. I'll never forgive myself.

Midwife crisis.

My wife is a data scientist and said I wasn't walking the dog enough and that she was doing most of them. Went through 12 months of our Strava stats and provided evidence that I was responsible for 60% of his walks. She threw a tantrum. Hasn't spoken to me in a week. I win.

That's why you should never data scientist.

My boyfriend bites his nails and leaves sharp edges on them. When he gives me a handjob, he keeps scratching me and my dick is often left in tatters. I love him but I'm going to break up with him.

Edward Jizzerhands

Thou Shalt Use These Shonky Tips

People tell us that the main

reason they read Fesshole is

for the shoplifting tips,

but oh, there is so much more.

Every month, for years, I book a day off work and do something fun: indoor climbing, kayaking, art lesson etc. I don't tell my wife anything about it. She thinks I've had a boring day at the office.

I'm in two separate 'Sports' WhatsApp groups, with different lads in each. Each group has one very knowledgable person with intelligent and interesting takes on football etc. I copy their comments and post them in the other group. Each group think I know my stuff. I haven't a clue.

I've done stand-up comedy for 12 years. After I've done a gig, I email the promoter pretending to be a member of the audience, asking when 'that brilliant comedian' will be back, as I want to bring 'all my friends' to watch him. Been re-booked so many times doing this.

Me and the wife control the house temperature from the Hive app. She's a stickler for not going above 17. When I'm working from home and she's out, I put the thermostat in the fridge but keep it at 17 so my use of extra heating goes unnoticed.

How to Blackmail

The secret to blackmailing people successfully is opening a huge Google form and asking them to tell you their confessions. However you can't all be amoral geniuses like us, so here are some other tips.

Started chatting to someone on Grindr. Swapped pics and discovered it was our 'straight' and married senior director from work. Got instantly blocked but have had the best pay rises over the last few years.

FAV: 8,232 RT: 97

When his skid marks are particularly bad, I've been taking pictures of my boyfriend's underwear on my phone. If he breaks up with me, I plan to share the photos with his friends.

FAV: 4,718 RT: 52

In 2003 I caught my brother wanking while cuddling the cat. I immediately blackmailed him into doing small jobs for me. Twenty years on he's married with kids and I can still get him to do the washing-up at Christmas by telling him it would be 'purrfect' if he could help.

FAV: 12,116 RT: 186

How to Save Money

We all need our money to go further – the trick is crime, lots of crime.

I've bought a gym membership so I can park there for less than the cost of parking in the town centre. It's also only a two-minute walk to work and five from my local pub. I've never been to the gym once and I've saved loads.

FAV: 19,413 RT: 412

I once sucked off a taxi driver for a lift home, but because it was an Uber I got charged anyway.

FAV: 11,397 RT: 247

Wife likes her tea weak, so I dunk her teabag a few times, then leave it by the jar for next time. I get 3-4 cups from each teabag. She hates that I do this, calls me a tightarse, but by my reckoning we save nearly £2 off grocery bills every year. Can't argue with those numbers.

FAV: 6,960 RT: 103

My girlfriend's parents are minted. Two years ago they bought us some things on Amazon and a takeaway on Just Eat at ours. Their card has been saved on my accounts ever since. I have ordered over £3,000 worth of food/items. They haven't even noticed.

FAV: 18,429 RT: 211

I have a habit of stealing
condiments from restaurants.
Ketchup, mustard, mayo – you
name it, I've taken it. I have a whole
drawer in my kitchen dedicated
to my stash of stolen sauces.
It's like my own personal
condiment black market.

FAV: 1,311 RT 27

Whenever I have to send someone money I always send up to £5 less than I was meant to. Almost everyone is too scared to sound like a tightarse to mention it. I put it all in a savings account. You'd be amazed how much I've 'saved' over the years.

During the cold spell in December I attended 3 funerals. I didn't know any of the deceased; however, the church and chapel were warm and there was a buffet afterwards.

Currently sat here in the airport departure lounge thanks to the thirsty guys of London. I set up a fake Tinder profile with an Insta model's photos with a bio asking for £10 to my Cash App to show you're actually serious. Five weeks and £470 later I'm on my way to Ibiza.

How to Save Money in Shops

Remember it's not shoplifting if you accidentally forget to scan it.

If anything breaks outside of its warranty I order it again off Amazon and return the broken item. I figure Jeff is too rich to notice or care.

My wife and kids claim to hate the Aldi knock-off cereals, and only eat the expensive ones. Little do they know they've been eating the Aldi ones for years, decanted into posh packaging.

FAV: 11,807 RT: 137

When shopping I swap the cardboard sleeves over on ready meals, so I pay value prices for the finest, most expensive dinners.

FAV: 9,258 RT: 118

Whenever I stay in a nice hotel, I take their shampoo. Now that most places have gone green, with large bottles screwed to the wall, I bring my own smaller container and patiently decant it. Probably take £10 value every stay. I'm mostly bald and make £800,000 a year.

FAV: 7,818 RT: 129

I'd quit shoplifting for years but was pulled back in by an ironing board, which I made multiple attempts to purchase through one of those self-scanners, drunk. In the end I just brazenly walked out with it, held like a surfboard and unpaid through sheer frustration.

FAV: 3,437 RT: 26

One Christmas in the mid-90s when I was absolutely skint and working in a sports shop, I had no choice but to steal all of my family's Christmas presents from our stock room. I'll never forget the look on my nan's face when she opened a full Reebok tracksuit.

FAV: 5,124 RT: 92

Evil Genius

Some evil is so genius that you can't help but take your hat off and be impressed – and these are the people who'd probably steal your hat and sell it back to you.

As a youngster I learned all the Monopoly Chance and Community Chest cards so I could read out a good one if I drew a bad one and just sneak it to the bottom of the deck

FAV: 3,725 RT: 44

I own a restaurant. When starting up I would make ghost bookings at all the restaurants nearby. They would turn away customers saving space for my fake bookings. Those extra customers might have kept me afloat in the beginning.

FAV: 10,807 RT: 163

I work at a posh school that requires us to wear academic gowns on occasions. All the other staff spent hundreds of pounds on theirs. I bought a cape from a magic shop.

FAV: 31,515 RT: 552

I'm somewhat of a prepper but don't have nearly enough money to get real about it. Instead, I follow a lot of preppers from my local area on social media who are not wise enough to mask their location. I've got a map on my wall with all the best spots should shit hit the fan.

FAV: 11,702 RT: 291

When I worked away I had to submit receipts for food to get reimbursed. I used to buy the wank mag *Nuts* and claim it back as food expenses, as that is how it appeared on the receipt. At least I know what it feels like to be an MP, even if it was just £1 a month.

FAV: 3,165 RT: 47

When I was a lad I wrote my brother's name on the wall in marker pen. He got a right shouting at by my parents saying, 'Who else would write YOUR name on the wall?' I never fessed up.

FAV: 3,816 RT: 33

When my mate's bit on the side told him she was going round to his house later that evening to tell his wife everything, he paid me £50 to let myself into his house and play the part of 'wife', while he took actual wife out for the night. It worked a treat.

FAV: 16.1k RT: 265

My Mrs has bought most of my Christmas presents off Amazon which is linked to my iPad. I see everything she buys. I haven't told her, it lets me know the level I need to be at for her gifts.

FAV: 3,270 RT: 20

I've developed a thing for gatecrashing luxury hotel spas. I walk in confidently, sign in as Mr M Smith from room 206, collect a free towel and luxuriate. I do this in the best hotels in the country and I've yet to be caught. The buzz is so good, I'm worried I have a problem.

FAV: 9,865 RT: 119

I'm a Vicar in the C of E. I use ChatGPT
to write my sermons and – according to
multiple parishioners – I'm preaching
brilliantly every week. I'd feel guilty but
the stipend is piss poor and this frees
up many hours per week to actually do
proper pastoral parish work. Fuck it.

I deliberately wrap my wife's Christmas presents badly so she never asks me to help wrap any of our children's presents each year. Works every time.

Every birthday and Xmas I give my spoilt step-daughter a gift card for £50 that I never actually activate at the till – so it has no money pre-loaded onto it whatsoever. I know she loses them or can't be bothered, and she's never said anything to me.

My wife fell in love with a dog from the dog's home. I paid staff an extra £10 if they told my wife it had a flatulence problem. We've now got the dog and I can silently release anytime I want and know the dog will get the blame.

My wife sent me out to buy a cordless razor for her father's birthday. I knew he did not have long to live, so I chose a really expensive one, knowing full well that I would get it when he died.

How to Make Money the Easy Way

House prices through the roof, inflation biting, so how can you earn an honest crust in these times? Go on the game, my son.

Wish I'd known about selling my breast milk to perverts earlier.

I found some car keys on the ground in a car park. Before handing them in to lost property, I swapped their Clubcard key ring for a spare one of mine so they'd rack up points for me.

My parents think my writing career has really taken off. What they don't know is I'm one of the top five authors in a very niche corner of the fetish erotica world. Took Mom on vacation to tour old churches using royalties from a lesbian domination ageplay book.

My girlfriend is really proud of me for getting several pay rises over the last year, whereas I've actually started an OnlyFans and been doing live cam shows for a largely gay male audience and it's going really well.

Got a side project going called 'cunt stock' which is investing in the worst companies imaginable – arms manufacturers, businesses that still test on animals, News Corp. Pleased but also ashamed to say that this is vastly outperforming my 'normal' investments.

I randomly pop into coffee shops and ask if anyone handed in a charger. I've collected four mobile phone chargers and two laptop chargers. Don't know what to do with them.

How to Save Money in Hotels

Hotels make too much money anyway. It's your moral imperative to walk off with those tiny shampoos.

I work away a lot. I looked up the price of lovely lush hotel pillows in my room: £80 x 4. The next time I stayed I did a swap with my cheapo ten-year-old dregs.

I've never paid extra for the cooked buffet at Premier Inn. Just pay for the continental food and go at a busy time and scoff as much sausage and bacon as you can. They never check.

I and my dog – an inherited Labrador – live in a tiny flat in London. I only have a small shower, so once a month I book a hotel in London that has a bath so I can bathe my dog. Most hotels don't allow pets so I told them I am a guide dog trainer. I'm in their company magazine.

Straight-up Advice For You to Live a Better Life

Straight-up tips to improve your life right now. Ours would be that buying socks is the one bit of retail therapy with tangible benefits: you have nice clean new socks.

I answer my front door in my coat. If it's someone I want to see I say I've just got in and if it's someone I really don't want to see, I say I was just on my way out. Works every time.

FAV: 11,141 RT: 302

I save a fortune by always carrying a portable mobile-signal jammer with me. I go out for a meal, ask for the bill and when it comes I turn on the jammer. This stops their PDQ working, meaning they can't take payment with cards. After about 20 minutes they give up and it's a freebie.

FAV: 15,101 RT: 239

Whenever I used to post a question I needed the answer to online, I'd scarcely get a response. Now, I also use an alternative account to reply with a horrendously wrong answer. I get dozens of responses under my wrong answer. People love correcting others and proving them wrong.

FAV: 6,486 RT: 167

I haven't listened to a voicemail since 2017. I run a multimillion-pound property fund and probably get 10–20 voicemails a day. If it's important, I assume they'll call back or email.

FAV: 3,828 RT: 40

My mum was moaning that people kept parking over her drive but the council refused to act on it. I found road paint on eBay and made a nice double yellow line in the dead of night using a cardboard stencil. She still thinks the council changed their mind.

FAV: 3,801 RT: 25

I hide chocolate, sweets and other things I don't want to share with my family in a tampon box. My husband doesn't look in there either. It's my secret stash and I'm really proud of it.

FAV: 3,040 RT: 35

How to Troll Like a Troll Master

Being an arsehole on the internet used to be a pastime for a select few nerds, but now it's the sport in danger of replacing rimming as the nation's favourite hobby.

I regularly make up implausible stories and situations and post them on the 'Am I being unreasonable?' forum on Mumsnet. Two have ended up in the *Daily Mail*. Passes the time on my daily commute.

FAV: 5,995 RT: 69

I colourised and 'shaved' a photo of Hitler and used it to create a free account on a dating site. He got a lot of messages. I didn't dare reply to any of them.

FAV: 3,313 RT: 60

My former workplace never changed the Twitter password after I left. Several months later, on a busy weekend, I tweeted from their account, asking customers to show that tweet to the admissions team to get free entry. It caused chaos and the management had to honour it.

FAV: 3,694 RT: 37

I take great pleasure in joining random Facebook groups for streets or estates, saying some highly triggering things like 'Have you seen that the man at number 20 is fly-tipping!' and then watching the world burn. Then I leave.

FAV: 6,855 RT: 134

I got banned from the Vanish Tip Exchange website for posting fake tips. Highlights included rubbing olive oil into a red-wine-stained carpet or undiluted orange squash into a butter stain on a polo shirt.

FAV: 3,819 RT: 73

How to Troll in the Real World

Expert trolls leap out of the internet and do it in the real world. The naughty scamps.

I listed a free 50" plasma TV on Freecycle just to see what would happen. Everything kicked off, the admin for my area tried to get it for himself and he got sacked.

FAV: 3,128 RT: 45

I put a fake planning notice on the lampposts on our street, saying the local school was closing and being turned into a migrant centre. The WhatsApp group went fucking mental.

FAV: 19,255 RT: 551

I put my non-recycling bin out at two in the afternoon, the day before collection. The neighbours followed my lead. I knew it was recycling/cardboard and swapped it under cover of darkness. The panic on our street this morning was hilarious.

FAV: 7,046 RT: 147

I had an old piano that I couldn't get rid of. One night some friends and I shoved it in their van and left it in the local town with a note on it that said 'Please play me.' It's still there six months later and the locals still think it's one of those council initiatives.

FAV: 4,888 RT: 99

Years ago, my friend doctored Mark Ronson's Wikipedia page to say that he'd written the theme tune to *Thundercats* when he was nine years old. Then we watched as it was quoted as truth by various journalists.

FAV: 3,658 RT: 95

Came home pissed one night and swapped over a Tory neighbour and a Labour neighbour's support boards. Got woken next morning to them arguing in the street blaming each other.

FAV: 3,572 RT: 50

Petty Revenge

Maybe you're someone who can't think up their own ideas for petty revenge. Well, even if you're not, you still can rejoice in other's petty bullshit.

Whenever I'm out and have my son in the pram and I see a car parked on a pavement, I always make an attempt to get past it, no matter how much I scratch it. Current record is both doors and a wing mirror.

FAV: 12,174 RT: 241

A woman who always argues in the local Facebook groups posted her address looking for her parcel. So I clicked on her profile, found her partner's name & sent him a Moonpig greetings card thanking him for a wonderful night and couldn't wait to see him again.

FAV: 11,715 RT: 177

An old woman sat in our pre-booked seats on the train, wouldn't shift. Husband and kids got moved to first class but I stayed as I'd noticed her shopping under the table. Spent the journey from London to Peterborough chewing gum and disposing of it in her brand-new clothes.

FAV: 18,211 RT: 173

I dislike my local binmen. Every so often when they piss me off, I take the dog for a walk at night and turn every bin so the handle faces away from the road. My record was over 250 bins.

FAV: 6,609 RT: 139

I was photographing
a wedding and a female guest
was exceptionally rude to me
and everybody else there, so
while editing, I made her teeth
banana yellow on every picture.

FAV: 12.7k RT: 214

A tight mate of mine on a shitty data plan keeps sending me videos and images on WhatsApp I have no interest in. I delete them and when he is at work I download them again so they rinse his data allowance by re-uploading them. I'm on unlimted data. He's on about 2GB or so.

At the gym changing room this morning, some tosser had his phone on loudspeaker, having a full-blown loud as fuck conversation while he got changed. I went over to use the hair dryer that was right next to him. He ended the call. I've never used a hair dryer previously. Victory.

Pranks for You to Try

Hello ghost of Jeremy Beadle, here's some ideas for your new TV series.

Partner is Italian. Her English is great but sometimes she struggles to find the right word for things. One day she asked me for the medical name for her private parts. I pranked her and thought nothing of it. Next day heard her on the phone to GP enquiring about her sore growler.

We have a wall filled with inspirational quotes at work. Months ago I slowly began removing the generic statements and replacing them with Captain Kirk phrases from *Star Trek*. No one has noticed.

I spread a rumor the new vending machine in the staff canteen is voice activated. For about 2 weeks people were trying to get it working with phrases like 'B7, Coke Zero', until an update in the weekly company newsletter confirmed it's just a normal vending machine.

FAV: 10,621 RT: 233

When farewell cards were passed around the office I used to use a different pen and write confounding messages from made-up people. 'Bye John – I'll never forget our late night nude chess games. Love, Brian'.

FAV: 6,182 RT: 149

Aged 15, at King's Cross station in London. A woman in a hurry asked me and my mate, 'Is that the Northern Line?' pointing at a Scotland-bound train. We of course said yes. First stop York, we both hung around to watch the train leave. Slightly chuckle about it 20 years later.

FAV: 4,785 RT: 96

When shopping in budget supermarkets, I like to spot anyone acting like they are better than everyone else, and I will ask them for something, pretending I think they work there. Their horror at the mere suggestion makes my day.

FAV: 5,352 RT: 87

When we were kids in the 90s, we'd find common surnames in the phone book, ring them up and say, 'There's a backlog of Smiths in the phone book, would you be interested in changing your surname for £250.'

FAV: 3,205 RT: 44

Sometimes when the wife is out of the house I get the suitcases down and start pretending to pack stuff and leave them by the door. Nothing to do with the wife, it's just to fuck with the cat who hates it when we go on holiday.

When we replaced our kitchen countertops a few years ago, we found a void underneath. So we put a time capsule together and hid it for the next people who renovate. Oh, and we put a full-size fake skeleton in there too.

My wife bought a painting on holiday in South Africa. It hangs in our bedroom. Every week, our ten-year-old son moves it slightly so it is lopsided. His mum thinks the picture is haunted by a poltergeist. The boy has done this every week for two years and has yet to fess.

Pranks That Went Wrong

The thing about pranks is that they upset the victim. Use this imformation wisely – or just play pranks on people who deserve it, like Vladimir Putin or Lofty from EastEnders.

I found out I had an anal fissure after I sent a video of the shit coming out of my arse as a prank to my friend and he suggested I should see a doctor due to its colour.

My dad put my mum's phone in her coffin with her for her burial. About 3 months later I thought it would be funny to change her number on his phone to mine and I text him saying, 'Get me out of this fucking box!' He didn't see the funny side and didn't speak to me for almost a year.

FAV: 78,276 RT: 3,482

When my son was small and mischievous I would often threaten to ring Tony Blair in an attempt to rein him in; he would get upset and beg me not to. He's now a 17-year-old politics student and a staunch Conservative. I think I accidentally turned him Tory.

FAV: 14,003 RT: 270

While very drunk one Xmas Eve, my brother and I tweezered the crap unfunny jokes out of the crackers and replaced them with print-outs of slightly more ribald jokes about bestiality and famous nonces. Mother has not bought crackers from Waitrose since.

FAV: 8,731 RT: 165

Aged 13 in 1991, used my 50p tuckshop money to phone a bomb threat to the school office as I didn't revise for a French test. Police turn up and establish it was a hoax. Test still on, I failed it, plus had no sweets from tuckshop as spent 50p making call from phonebox. Karma fucked me.

FAV: 7,051 RT: 76

When I was younger I watched *Tom and Jerry* a lot and thought I would emulate them and I put some drawing pins in my father's slippers. Imagine my surprise when he came home from work and did not jump as high as the ceiling as Tom did, but grounded me for a week.

Revenge Served Cold

The best revenge is living well, but if you can't do that, fuck people up.

A van cut me up and stopped at the lights. I texted the number on the side, 'I know what you have done; the game is up.' Two days later he replied, 'I'm going to tell her everything, just give me a couple of days.'

Found the girl my boyfriend cheated on me with on Facebook. Turned out she still lived at home with her mum. Joined her mum's bookclub. Just so that I could be there when the girl came home with my ex.

I had an ex boyfriend who I've since realised made me miserable and I've blocked him on every channel possible. Whenever Liverpool lose I sign him up to emails from whichever club have beaten them. I've never been as busy as this season.

Got divorced 5 years ago and my ex-wife still hasn't realised that my Nectar card is linked to her eBay account. She uses eBay every day so has paid for my Christmas shop for the last 5 years.

I build custom wheelchairs. Recently had an incredibly rude customer who I overheard using racist language when he thought I couldn't hear. So I made one of his wheels slightly smaller than the other. Fucker is going round in circles for the rest of his life.

When I sold my house, the buyer was such a despicable human during the process. I took great pleasure in removing a few of the brackets from some kitchen cupboards, so that they couldn't put any of their things in there without the shelf falling over.

Hobby and Project Ideas

Fancy spinning up your own hit internet project? Well, the trick is to think of something that people do already and then industrialise the process: so if you like farting, then open a version of Spotify for botty burps.

I keep two tally charts in my work notebook. No one knows about it, but it's to do with the number of times I initiate sex with my wife and how many times she initiated it. I'm currently on 43, she's on 3.

The letters 'LP' appeared in yellow spray paint up and down our street one afternoon. My pal reckoned they were for new lamp posts and we wondered what would happen if we added a few more. Thirty years later the street still has a ridiculous amount of lighting.

I have a New Year's Resolution to do 1,000 shits in a year. It works out at 2.8 shits a day. I have even made a spreadsheet for it. I am averaging 2.6 a day at the moment and reckon if I work hard I can climb the shitty mountain to 1,000 shits in 2023.

The Secret Games You Play

Bored? Here's some tips to help you while away your time with 'games', and that doesn't include pocket billiards.

Occasionally I walk around my home with my eyes closed to see if I would be able to cope if I suddenly became blind. So far the results:
Stubbed toes: 16
Smashed foreheads: 5
Shame: none

A big hole has appeared in our local park and nobody knows how it got there. It's me. I go out every night after dark and dig it a little deeper.

Dad loves creepy charity shop portraits. I commissioned an artist friend to paint two of the same woman, only in one she's smiling. Gave Dad the other and he put it on the landing. Changed it for April Fool's and it shocked him so much he fell down the stairs and fractured his arm.

FAV:22,400 RT:745

While watching films in which the actors go underwater, I like to hold my breath to see if it is actually feasible for the amount of time. Damn near killed myself watching *Aquaman*.

When restaurant staff ask if I enjoyed my meal and it was bad, I'll tell them it was 'as good as my mum's cooking'. They always accept it as a compliment – it's very much not, my mum is a terrible cook.

I like to one-up people's email closings. If they say 'sincerely' I respond with 'very sincerely'. If they say 'warm regards' I respond with 'warmest regards'.

I always board planes last just to see the disappointment on the face of the person who thought they had a spare seat next to them.

I try to empty the dishwasher before the kettle boils in the morning. I often feel this is the only successful accomplishment of the day.

When I was younger, I deliberately swallowed a 5p coin just to see how long it would take to travel through my body. Hearing it ching against the toilet basin was utter fulfilment.

A decade ago I worked in a Tesco Express petrol station. A fellow cashier and I used to pretend we didn't have any £5 notes every Friday night and gave everybody all their change in coins. Whoever had the most £5 notes in the till at the end of the shift won.

FAV: 3,901 RT: 32

My wife and I created a people-watching game called 'Daughter or Midlife Crisis'. The rules are simple: any time you see a middle-aged man with a beautiful woman half his age, you need to work out if he's with his daughter or having a midlife crisis.

FAV: 8,308 RT: 198

My wife spent ages teaching the kids her mobile number so they could call her in an emergency from any phone. I just set mine as the password to the gaming PC. Same result, zero effort.

FAV:12,568 RT:320

For six years I have occasionally been going to a friend's house to play Scrabble. Each time I've taken along an extra E tile and added it to his set. He is now playing with nine extra Es. He hasn't actually noticed but complains about having too many Es every time.

FAV:10,213 RT:342

HAVE YOUR SAY

~~~~~~

People love replying to confessions like Victor Meldrew screaming 'I don't believe it!' but that's not the ones we're printing here because we haven't paid the rightsholders to use the catchphrase.

I like to do 'ethical shoplifting' where I take things from the shelves of big supermarkets and place them in their food bank baskets at the end of the store. Technically not stealing as the items never leave the premises – just moving them really.

Robin Hood and Lidl John

I live alone and when I moved into my apartment the bloke opposite made it clear he fancied me. I wasn't interested but when he asked me in for Thai food I saw it as an opportunity to take a photo of his wi-fi box. It's been over 2 years now, he's clueless and saved me about a grand.

All the girlies say I'm pretty Thai for a wi-fi

I'm a chef. I 'created' a soup du jour for our menu that goes out at £7.95. It's a can of Heinz + an Oxo cube + shitloads of water + cornflour + salt. I stick a basil leaf on it to make it look well posh. One can serves about 12. Three for £2 in Tesco.

The profit margins are huge! You must be a bouillonaire!

I'm a single woman, and any time I'm looking for a tradesman, I go on Tinder. Strike up a convo, few dates, job I couldn't get anyone for is done. Plumber, electrician, handyman, works a treat.

Screw/Fix

Thou Shalt Parent Like a Parenting Bastard

Parenting is tough – first they're little shits that take up all your time and you can't go to the pub, then you blink and they're full-grown adults draining your purse and telling you that the Stone Roses are shit and you're old and past it.

My wife, and indeed everyone, thinks our son's name is Steven. I actually got drunk before signing his birth certificate and changed it to Stevenage instead.

Just deep-throated the last chocolate eclair in the toilet so my husband couldn't have any.

My son plays football in a league for 7- and 8-year-olds. His team have a lot of fun but they are absolutely terrible. I make my wife take him now because watching such utter shit play stressed me out too much.

Just heard my wife tell our 6-year-old that her appalling behaviour is like Hitler, who only 'thought of himself'. Torn between being shocked to hear it as a parent and also thinking, as a historian, that it's a slightly unfair and mistaken representation of Hitler's motivations.

There's a group of 40-year-old women who give me the evil eye when I pick up my son, purely because I'm younger. Sometimes I'll put a tight outfit on solely to go and collect him in, because I take great pleasure in watching how irrated they get at their staring husbands.

My wife and I had a baby girl last week, and everybody keeps telling us how beautiful she is ... all I see is Ross Kemp. Don't all babies look like one of the Mitchell brothers?

When I go to feed my baby, I first offer him a sniff of the nursing pad from my bra, like a waiter offering a taste of the wine before pouring. I feel it adds a touch of class to having my tits out constantly.

I like it when my 7-year-old cries at sad moments in cartoons or TV programmes. It reassures me he's not going to be a sociopath when he grows up.

Parenting Life Hacks

The main parenting life hack you need is getting someone else to pay for it all – the sperm donors have a point.

Two years ago my wife cancelled Sky Sports and I started a long game. My 6-year-old son had never been into football and I started work subtly: playing footy in the garden with him, getting him playing in local team. Now he's just asked to watch on TV. Sky Sports reinstated. Job done.

I accidentally got my son free entry to the local swimming pool every week for a year because the young girl on the desk thought being 'adopted' was a disability.

I love my son, but can't stand reading bedtime stories. As a result, I cut them down to reduce the time commitment. His current favourites are *The Two Little Pigs* and *Snow White and the Dwarf*.

Some nights I tell my 5-year-old it's '1 minute to bedtime' an hour or so before bedtime. She sneaks off to play quietly on her own and I get some peace.

Last night my teenage son was being an utter arse and refused to come to an event we had booked. So I took the router along in his place; it had a seat, drink and chocolates and I even got some pics. Future dates may happen.

I set up a home speaker app which takes contentious family decisions for us. You can ask it to choose which takeaway we're having, or whose turn it is to do the dishes etc. I set it up to slightly favour my food choices and to rarely pick me for housework. The family has no clue.

Every New Year's Eve my daughter would want to stay up until 12, so I would play previous New Year countdowns on YouTube at 8pm and pretend she'd had a late night so that she would go to sleep and I could have some peace.

Doing Parenting Right

Some parents are twats, but some are heroes. Are you doing it right? Our tip is to give the kids some oven chips and hope for the best.

My kids expect a made-up story each night, be it about a fat useless butterfly, or fat useless slug, a fat useless dragon, a fat useless worm ... the story always ends the same way: 'and he grew up to be Boris Johnson'. They fucking love it.

> **I persuaded my wife not to tell her dad that her mum is having an affair, not because I care about the emotional outcome but because it'll nuke our free childcare.**
>

My 4-year-old daughter loves playing *Grand Theft Auto 5*. She stamps on pedestrians, shoots cops and causes diabolical levels of havoc. We only ever play while her mother is out so she has no clue her daughter is a Los Santos badass.

I give my 5-year-old son's toys silly voices while playing with him. This backfired when his teacher asked why he's greeting other kids at school with a spot-on Papa Lazarou 'HELLO DAVE'.

Told my daughter I could poo potatoes.
Took one to the loo one day and once
I'd done my No. 2, ran downstairs to
show her. Next day she told her teacher.
Made for an interesting parents' evening.
Been told I'm not allowed to bring it up in
the father of the bride speech.

FAV: 4,526 RT: 90

Every time I leave my 8-year-old son in a room when I've got a beer, I make a sneaky mark on the label where it's up to. When I return I always ask him if he's tried it. He always says no. The beer is always slightly below the mark. Little fucking legend.

Lies to Tell Kids

The ideal fib to tell kids is one that'll keep them quiet for a bit, like telling them there's a competition for who can be the quietest. This actually works. Try it.

I told my kids I went to Hogwarts. Then I turned the volume in the car up and down using my thumb on the steering wheel controls while waving my other hand up and down. Went on for years, they told teachers, friends and got quite cross if anyone doubted them.

We told our children that open-top sports cars were for poor people that couldn't afford four seats and a roof. Drivers of such cars were pitied for many years.

My dad gives my 4-year-old daughter a £10 note every time we visit. She prefers a 'gold coin' so I trade her.

Parenting Adult Kids

Just because they've left home doesn't mean the parenting stops. Or the hand-outs.

I pretend I don't understand computers and online banking, so I can call my son; just so I can make sure he visits and that he's doing OK.

FAV: 6,711 RT: 88

Sons have grown up and moved in with their partners. We've now downsized, primarily to free up money and live in a smaller, more manageable house. But also to discourage them from moving back in with us.

FAV: 5,036 RT: 44

When I pay for stuff for my grown-up kids, I always give them a 20 per cent discount without their knowledge when they pay me back because I can't quite believe they're functioning adults with proper jobs.

FAV: 3,106 RT: 33

I Saw Parents Shagging

Should you ever see your parents making sweet, sweet love, remember it's not OK to shout 'Room for one more?'

I once had a wank over the sound of my parents having sex. I thought it was the neighbours. I can never tell another soul.

FAV: 2,996 RT: 35

My 15-year-old son is now coming to the gym
with me. He's getting stronger but I can't
let the little bastard lift more than me.
Rotator cuff is stuffed, both knees are poked
and my back and hips constantly ache.
I live on pain killers and anti-inflammatory rub.

24 years ago, aged 18, I walked in on Dad licking Mum out after I'd been on a night out. Mum brought me a cup of tea the next morning and asked how my night was. Told her I didn't remember getting home, to save embarrassment. Still haunted to this day. Awful memory to have.

FAV: 24,522 RT: 330

As a kid I wandered into my parents' bedroom, opening drawers etc. Under their bed I found handcuffs, accidentally handcuffed myself and had to wait for my dad to get home to release me. It has only just occurred to me, 20 years later, why they were under their bed.

FAV: 3,979 RT: 61

Kids (and Parents) Say the Funniest Things

The funniest thing our kids say is, 'Yes dad, I have done my homework and I will look for a job.' Loooooooool.

Earlier this week, my 4-year-old daughter asked me while we were getting changed after swimming, 'Daddy, why is your penis so chunky?' I've never felt so flattered and horrified at the same time.

FAV: 7,080 RT: 65

My mum has started calling the cupboard under the stairs 'the glory hole'. It's just awful. I don't know how to react. Help!

FAV: 4,408 RT: 77

At a recent family gathering my two-year-old son bemused the crowd by repeatedly shouting 'Pickle Lane toy car'. I denied knowing what he was talking about. What they don't know is that on the way to the venue I had reason to shout 'Pick a lane, Tory cunt' at another road user.

I taught my niece to say 'I need to curl one out' when she needs a poo. My sister was not impressed when her nursery spoke to her about her daughter shouting that she needs to curl one out and teaching other kids.

I'm a lesbian and play the banjo. Once my mum bought me a shoulder strap for it. Later when I visited her, she asked if I had my strap on. I stared at her in horror for a few seconds before realising what she meant.

Punishing Kids for Fun and Pleasure

If you can't bully little humans smaller than yourself, then what is even the point of being a big human?

I report the profiles of all my under-13-year-old family members and friends' kids on social media so that their accounts can be closed, as they're not old enough. Some get really upset but I enjoy it.

When my 10-year-old insisted she was fine wearing shorts and a T-shirt in sub-freezing weather I intentionally parked at the far end of the parking lot and slow-walked to our destination. It was disturbingly satisfying.

I hated peas as a child so my mother would hide a pea in my roast dinners every sunday. Every week I would finish my dinner, then victoriously leave the solitary pea alone on the plate. I'm 44 now and yesterday she confessed that she actually used to hide two peas. The twat.

A child kept kicking my seat on a long-haul flight back to London, and his mother refused to stop him or apologise. When she took him to the loo I poured water into his seat. She soon thought he'd wet himself. Served him right.

My kids refused to clean up their Xmas Lego properly, so I hoovered up bits of it and emptied the bag into the big bin. Let's see them rebuild their Lego city street scene now.

My 11-year-old son gets £7.50 a week pocket money. I tax and NI him and he also has to save 20 per cent each week so he's left with about 4 quid. He hates the tax man already and he's now starting to hate the government. May as well start them early.

Revenge on Family

Revenge is a dish best served cold to family members so they can choke on the gristle in the trifle.

I really dislike my dad, so play the same lotto numbers. If he wins he's not having it all to himself.

FAV: 4,425 RT: 50

As a child, I had a fine system for my parents. I'd take a quid out of either of their wallets if they upset me. This week, I've been staying with them for work and they've been pissing me off. The fine system is back and this time it's a fiver.

FAV: 4,229 RT: 46

Father-in-law is a money bore – five minutes into any family visit he'll inform us how rich he is. Every time I'm at his house, I take every chargeable electrical device I own and charge them up on his dime.

FAV: 3,872 RT: 28

I Love Being a Dad

Plenty of people love being a parent – it's probably Stockholm syndrome, mind you.

I feel like I have to do Serious Dad Voice when I catch my nine-year-old sneakily reading in his room way, way after his bedtime. I'm always absolutely delighted.

FAV: 7,925 RT: 77

Picked my nearly 3-year-old up from nursery today.
When I carried her back to the car, she gave me a
massive kiss on the cheek and said, 'Missed you
Dad, love you,' and ... well, it's probably one of the
best things thats happened to me. Wife would be so
jealous if she knew.

My mates think I'm under the thumb because I don't
go to the pub anymore, but it's because I choose to
play iPad games to earn 'coins' that my little boy can
spend on shiny new cars or characters or whatever.
I like him more than I like any of them.

I'm a dad of three grown-up daughters and each of
them secretly says to me, 'I know I'm your favourite,'
and I always tell them, 'Yes, but don't tell the others.'

My infant son has trouble sleeping without one of us in
bed with him. I grumble about it but I secretly love it. He
doesn't hog the bed and I know one day he won't want
to have anything to do with me. His joy when he sees me
makes life worth living

My husband is banned from the cinema after loudly
uttering 'It needs to be deeper, a dog will dig that up'
during the burial of Dobbie.

Kids' Names

If you're stuck for a name for a child, pick your favourite pin-up and mix it with the surname from your favourite murderer. Well it worked OK for the parents of Marilyn Manson and he ended up on Top of the Pops.

I named my son Edward after Edward Elizabeth Hitler from *Bottom*. I can now shout Eddie at him in Richie's voice with impunity.

FAV: 3,473 RT: 108

I'm a massive Oasis fan and managed to convince my wife to name our daughter Violet, as we both love the song 'Songbird' and I always liked the lyric 'she's a little violet in my mind'. Violet is now five and found out three weeks ago that the lyric is 'she's a little pilot'.

FAV: 9,453 RT: 203

The First Rule of Dad Club

...is if someone says 'stop' or goes limp, taps out, the Dad is over.

On the morning school run, once I've dropped off my son, I drive past another dad. We always look out for each other and exchange a wave. Every morning for five years now. We've never spoken a word, don't know each other's names but that wave to my mate brings me happiness each morning.

FAV: 14,446 RT: 128

Proud of My Sprogs... I Think

The small joys of parenthood when they do something useful like getting a job and earning enough money to buy you a pint.

His confession really, but my 6-year-old son just attempted to create a stink bomb by taking off a sock, farting on it and then throwing it at his sister. Truly disgusting, but I love his ingenuity.

FAV: 5,445 RT: 101

Our son showed us his box full of dildos the other day and it's hard to navigate the very complex territory between 'Why would you show us that?' and 'We're glad you feel able to show us that.'

FAV: 8,243 RT: 139

My Dad Watched a Porno

Porn is a fact of life. Your mum probably watches it too but she's cleverer than Dad and can delete the search history on her phone.

My parents shared an iPad. When I was 14 my mum confronted me in front of Dad about the open tabs of porn on it. I lied and said it had been me. Guess who quietly got £100 from their dad that night?

FAV: 9,272 RT: 77

My dad gave me his Amazon account so I can order some stuff on his Prime. What he doesn't know is that I can see his recent orders which included an anal training kit and one of those lock things you put over your dick. I'm trying my hardest to forget what I saw.

FAV: 3,641 RT: 59

My dad isn't terribly computer literate, so he asked me to investigate why his laptop was running slow. Almost immediately discovered a history full of 'granny porn' searches – am torn between horror at the discovery and relief that his interests are age appropriate.

Awkward Interactions Between Family and Sex

Sex should never be discussed between children and parents, it's embarrassing for everyone. Just tell your kids you got them off eBay or something and nothing has happened downstairs since 1976 anyway.

I often help my elderly parents on their computer. The other day I had to find a webpage they'd been on that day to buy something. Turns out my 81-year-old dad has been absolutely smashing gay porn while my mum is out. Can't look him in the eyes, and he can't spell twink.

Only me and mother-in-law in house. Told her I was going to have a bath. Decided to have a crafty phone wank. Couldn't work out why there was no sound. Turned it up full blast. Nothing. Went back downstairs. Phone was connected to Alexa's Bluetooth. We have never spoken of this.

Returning home from college, I struggled to get my key in the front door lock. After much force, I managed to get in. Halfway up the stairs I saw my dad in his bedroom using the Dyson to suck himself off and immediately realised why he'd left the key in the lock. Scarred for life.

Wife and I plucked up the courage to attend a suburban swingers' party. Arrived at the venue only to see parked in the driveway my recently widowed mum's car. She clocked us arriving in our car, so we just drove on. Never spoke of it again. And still never been to a sex party.

My and my partner made a video one night, you know the kind. Anyway, our 6-year-old daughter had recently got a new iPad and somehow had the same photos and videos. One day she came back from Nan's excitedly telling us she had watched us wrestling, and so had Nan. Mortified.

Back in the day I kept stealing condoms from my parents so I could have a posh wank every now and then. I stopped when I overheard my mum telling a friend she suspected my dad was having an affair because the condoms kept reducing too quickly.

HAVE YOUR SAY

~~~~~~

Here's some of the best comments in reply to fesses that aren't lazy fuckers getting that terrible GPT-4 bot to write their replies for them.

My wife and I have a daughter named Katherine. Or Catherine. I can't remember which we chose. She's going to be 1 soon and I don't feel like I can ask.

If only there was some kind of official document you could check.

My son took his first steps in the living room with me while my wife was working late. That evening we watched together as our son took his first steps. A magical moment that she has treasured for years.

You take that to your GRAVE

I have five toes. My husband has five toes but my daughter has six, as does our next-door neighbour. Hope my husband never spots him wearing flip-flops one of these days.

I only have four on my left foot. It repulsed my ex-wife. She's lack-toes intolerant.

Found out hubby was on dating sites, made some fake profiles he matched with and talks to. Mainly it's about how he misses the intimacy and closeness now we have three kids and busy lives. Sometimes I wish I could tell him he's confiding in me..

Ask him if he likes pina coladas and getting caught in the rain.

Thou Shalt Have a Brain Completely Consumed by Sex

Britain is filthy.

And that's not just because

you don't wash,

you're <u>obsessed</u> with sex,

wanking and smut.

It's like Carry On Jizzing

with you lot.

If I'm in bed and want a drink, I'll have sex with the husband, he'll go downstairs for a fag afterwards, I'll ask him to bring a glass of water up.

Since getting our Tesla I can see on the app exactly where my husband is having sex with men: lay-bys, cemeteries and the occasional house visit. I'll often pass sanctimonious judgement on closeted married men who cheat on their wives just to enjoy his fake reaction.

The satisfaction on my wife's face when she successfully cuts an entire sheet of wrapping paper just by sliding the scissors beats anything I've ever been able to provide her.

Sex Gone Wrong

If you're missing out on sex, here's some handy reminders that you're only missing out on humiliation and embarrassment.

Started seeing a stunning woman. Few weeks in, book dirty weekend away in fancy hotel. First night I'm in bed naked and she's undressing. I slide across bed for my mobile and leave a 1m long skid mark across the sheet. She's in a taxi home half an hour later and I never see her again.

I heard my neighbour moaning one morning and had a wank listening to her. Found out later she was out and it was a pigeon.

FAV: 16,856 RT: 579

My girlfriend is a nurse and was fingering my arse last night. She informed me halfway through I had a haemorrhoid. Ruined the moment.

FAV: 11,534 RT: 251

I was staying in a hotel and brought a girl back. She said she was going to freshen up and gave me a wink. I heard the tap come on and thought she was planning sex in the shower so I burst in. She was having a shit and had turned on the tap to cover the noise.

FAV: 13,240 RT: 229

Met the most beautiful girl at a bar. Somehow pulled her. Took her back to mine. Moved to the stand and carry and she came really quickly – and as she did, she shit all over my dick, balls and legs. Covered in it. I had to change carpets. Married her. We don't EVER talk about it.

FAV: 18,097 RT: 270

I went out with a guy once that I met on a BDSM website. He was a Dom and I was to be his Sub. Looking back, he just wanted me to do his shopping – at my expense – and I've only just realised 15 years later.

FAV: 5,533 RT: 88

During a power cut my wife and I had a marathon sex session. Woke up in the morning, went for a wee, only to see my cock was practically black. I screamed, presuming I had somehow killed it, only to realise that in the dark my wife had reached for lube but used fake tan.

Got a wank off a girl wearing a big ring. Rubbed my bellend so raw it looked like Gorbachev's head.

I met a woman in Edinburgh via a dating site for no-strings-attached fun while there for work. Had a great 90 minutes of very energetic sex, she was extremely horny and adventurous. When we finished I noticed an urn on the bedside table. Her husband's ashes – cremated the previous Thursday.

I once put one of my wife's dildos up my ass while she was out. Was horrified to see my teenage son had come home without hearing him and he stood there looking at me. Two years later and we still can't look at each other.

In the heat of the moment, I randomly sucked my girlfriend's toes the other night for the first time during sex. She got really turned on and now wants me to do it every time. I hated it, they tasted like Quavers.

Sexy Talk Gone Wrong

If you want to introduce sexy talk into the bedroom our advice is to say French things like 'le Eiffel Tower' and 'riots'.

After sex I place a single tissue over my knob to make it look like a little ghost. I shout 'woooo' at my girlfriend and twitch it about. She says she's going to leave me if I do it again. I'm going to to it again.

FAV: 15,368 RT: 394

I was once having amazing sex with a guy. Like top tier. We're getting fully into it and naturally started changing positions. As we moved, he suddenly shouted out 'AUTOBOTS TRANFORM!'. Safe to say I didn't finish.

FAV: 10,768 RT: 370

> **During the World Cup my boyfriend was fingering me after some hot sex. Just as I was about to cum, he whispered in my ear, 'This one's for the Three Lions'. I lost my orgasm and I've genuinely never despised someone/football more.**
>
> FAV: 20,562 RT: 474

My husband insists upon calling my penis a willy and it's completely killed our sex life.

FAV: 3,724 RT: 43

During the early 2000s, I went through a stage of saying 'Ahhhh Bisto' everytime I cum after sex. Girlfriend hated it.

FAV: 4,175 RT: 104

My girlfriend and I like to role-play.
She suggested we play the angry
farmer and the naughty sheep.
She even bought herself a rubbish
sheep costume. It was going well
but as she climaxed she shouted
'BAA', put me right off.

Popped into a massage joint for a happy ending earlier. Beautiful Polish girl is tugging away when out of the blue she asks, 'Are you ready for Christmas?' Nothing could have put me off more as I grunted, 'Still got a couple of gifts to buy.'

Tried to talk dirty to my wife to initiate sex and attempted Danny Dyer's line in *Human Traffic*: 'I can't wait to see your fanny.' She was horrified. Didn't get laid.

Slept with a girl recently and halfway through, with an angry face, she shouted, 'FILL ME UP' – I couldn't help picturing putting fuel in my car. Quickly finished and drove home laughing all the way.

Once got fingered by a trainee doctor. He asked afterwards if I was constipated, as he could feel it during the act. Never took him up on that second date and purchased some Lactulose instead.

Role-playing sexy Italian for my wife and asked, 'You wanna I licka the pussy?' Apparently I sounded like the Dolmio puppet, so she said no.

My teenage son thinks I don't
know about the phallic-shaped
vegetables disappearing from the
fridge and turning up in the bin.
I'm grateful he throws them away
afterwards rather than putting
them back but I don't like the waste.
I'm wondering if I should offer
to buy him a dildo.

Oral Sex Gone Wrong

The trick to doing blow jobs right is to imagine it's a recorder and mime the fingering for God Save the Queen.

Took a girl home one night at uni and she gave me a goodbye blowjob the next morning. When I spunked, she casually stood up, opened my skylight window and spat it out on the roof, like it was the done thing. I could see the stain for months afterwards.

FAV: 4,907 RT: 48

Had a terrible cold but still went down on the wife. After I made her cum she was rubbing herself gently, 'Wow, you've made me wetter than I've ever been, I think.' I was very proud of myself, despite knowing most of it was the snot from my runny nose.

FAV: 7,061 RT: 115

Group Sex Gone Wrong

The best-sized group for sex is two, because we're Victorian prudes and also quite honestly no group has asked us yet. Although if they did ask, we'd choose Bananarama.

Me and my girlfriend were drunk in a Spoons and a guy tried to hit on her and asked if she would join him in the mens. I dared her to, thinking it would be erotic and she sucked him off and now our relationship has never been the same.

FAV: 4,773 RT: 93

I'm a straight woman and I lived with my soon-to-be-ex-husband and new boyfriend for three months. While you might think this was all glorious steamy nights of sexy threesomes, in reality it meant I spent twice as much time putting the fucking loo seat down.

FAV: 3,105 RT: 51

I once had a threeway with a couple. They decided to put an Elton John compilation album on in the background. It felt ridiculous to be eating her out to 'The Circle of Life' but I didn't want to ruin the mood.

FAV: 3,225 RT: 63

I go to swingers' clubs on my own and every time think I'm going to have sex with all the women. Instead I shrivel in confidence and awkwardly just have tea/coffee in a towel and never do anything.

FAV: 4,155 RT: 46

When I was 24 I went to my first orgy with my girlfriend. It wasn't until we saw her parents in the corner that it became our last.

FAV: 10,505 RT: 217

Managed to talk my girlfriend into becoming swingers because I wanted to fuck other girls. Went to one and she got mullered by about 10 different cocks while no woman even looked at me. She's desperate to go back. Worst thing I've ever done.

FAV:10,156 RT:232

Men Who Are Deluded About Their Own Chances for Sex

Men are always hopeful and there's nothing more hopeful than a middle-aged man 'flirting' with waiting staff.

I'm a married man, overweight and balding. Whenever an attractive woman is nice to me, I become convinced that she has fallen in love with me and will want to sleep with me. So far, this is yet to happen, but I continue on with this inner delusion.

FAV: 6,424 RT: 71

I'm 44, overweight and married. The girl who hands over my Morrisons click & collect order in the car park every weekend just saw me in the store, made eye contact and smiled at me. I've now spent all day plotting how to leave my wife for her, as we clearly have an unspoken connection.

FAV: 4,850 RT: 49

> **I always wear my best socks and pants when I know the girl I fancy in work is in the office, just in case I ever get lucky with her. I'm a fat, balding, middle-aged, married father of two.**
>
> FAV: 5,334 RT: 60

I discovered cheese at a very young age, but when I look back at all the Beefeater meals I had as a young teenager, thinking I was sophisticated ordering the cheese board for dessert, thinking the waitresses would fancy me, I realise I was just a twat.

FAV: 5,638 RT: 43

Sex Tips

If you want some tips on how to do sex better: men, tidy up more.
Women: do whatever you like, men are just grateful that it happens.

My husband doesn't believe in lube or foreplay and just
sticks it in dry. I have to let out a bit of wee onto him so it
doesn't feel like someone's shoving a rough parsnip into
me. He thinks he gets me wet all by himself.

FAV: 10,174 RT: 160

**My wife has developed a Mr Tumble kink. Watching
that stupid twat on the TV is bad enough, but now at
least once a week I have to dress up as him and give
her 'tumble time'. Making me want to leave her tbh.**

FAV: 6,730 RT: 199

A girl I fancied at school loved *EastEnders*. At a school
disco I spray painted 'Free Arthur Fowler' on a wall,
despite never watching it or knowing the storyline, just
what I'd overheard. I was rewarded with a blow job on the
bus home.

FAV: 3,253 RT: 50

**Every time the weather turns to thunder and
lightning me and my girlfriend have a shag and
pretend we're conceiving the antichrist**

FAV: 5,439 RT: 174

If it's been a while since I've had sex, I go and hang out in hotel bars which are always full of men working away from home. Get laid every single time with minimal effort from my side, and always no strings attached as they're likely married.

When I have sex with my husband, I think of Skeletor from *He-Man* and it always makes me cum. Just praying I never accidentally shout out his name.

Sexy Games Gone Too Far

If you want to spice things up in the bedroom, why not try sticking a bay leaf on your genitals?

Standing naked in the bathroom, about to get in the shower in front of my wife, I had a fart brewing. To put on a show I squatted to let it out in all its glory and shat on the bath mat. Five years later I'm getting divorced, can't help but feel this incident may have caused it.

Met a girl in a bar in Dublin. Went outside in the alley to get it on. She thought it was 'hot' that I wasn't wearing underwear. Didn't have the heart to tell her I'd discarded my pants when I shat them in a farting competition 30 minutes previously.

Begged my girlfriend for months to peg me with a strap-on. She finally agreed. I shat the bed while she was ramming me, she was sick over my back when she pulled out. We haven't touched each other since, pretty sure she's going to leave me.

Sex Now That I Am Not as Young as I Once Was

Just becase you've got large adult kids doesn't mean you should stop the bedroom badminton.

Bought some sex straps and learned various knots to spice things up in the bedroom. Used once for the deed. Mainly used now to strap bags of frozen goods to various limbs for pain relief.

I give the kids jobs and tasks to keep them busy while me and the wife sneak off to have sex. I was mid-thrust when I thought about all those times I was sent to the shops as a kid for a paper that went straight in the bin when I got back. I've never gone soft so fast in my life.

After the death of my partner, I visited sex workers. One such lady asked what my kink was and I just wanted to say, 'Put on some flannel pyjamas, fire up the hot water bottle, and let's watch an episode of *Grace and Frankie*' but I was too ashamed to ask for it.

**My relationship with my
ex-husband started to go
downhill when I came home
from work early to surprise him,
and caught him having gay
sex dressed as a furry.**

For 10 years my husband has wanted me to poo on him in bed. I've always said no because I think it's disgusting. About two weeks ago, I gave in and did it. It was completely disgusting, he looked repulsed, barely touched it and neither of us has mentioned it since.

My husband keeps asking me to roleplay as a slug in the bedroom, he keeps stressing that it has to be a slug not a snail. I don't know what I'm meant to do.

Wife has a fetish for the puppets Sooty and Sweep. She has me wear them on my hands as I'm going down on her. I always put on a little show on her belly to make her laugh, though it annoys me how hard it is to do Sweep's voice with a mouthful of minge.

Husband nagged me to do anal for years. I finally gave in one night and purposefully shat all over his cock and balls. It was like 'a torrent of chocolate pudding' according to him. He's never asked since, the pervy pushy bastard.

The wife wanted to experiment in the bedroom the other day. She wanted me to dress up as a clown and to honk a horn to inform her before I came. We did it and will never speak of it ever again.

Getting out of shower, decided wife should be greeted with a helicopter/spinning dick dance as she walked in. Only it was our 12-year-old daughter. I don't think we can ever speak again.

FAV: 12,814 RT: 215

Sex Accidentally Involving Dogs

Our advice is not to have sex with dogs. Not unless you give them a biscuit first

As a teen, I'd let my dog lick up the 'mess' after wanking. Every time he went to the vet, I was terrified they would diagnose him with some ailment that could only be caused by ingesting semen.

FAV: 5,712 RT: 77

Pulled. Went back to her place. She had a yappy terrier that kept getting in way, so kept pushing him off mid-action. As we got near end, had to pull out. Managed to go all over the dog. She was hurt I didn't want a relationship, but how could I when I'd jizzed on her dog's face?

FAV: 3,253 RT: 67

The dog has ruined my sneaky wanks. After I knock one out, he relentlessly sniffs my crotch. The wife twigged it when he started sniffing both our crotches after sex.

FAV: 4,077 RT: 36

Why We're Not Having Sex Anymore

----

*The problem of getting older is unless you're very lucky,
your partner will probably go off sex. That's why the correct
response is taking up sniffing glue.*

**I'm being cockblocked by my dog – every night he
races me to bed and gets cuddles with the wife. I'll
get the last laugh though when the vet chops his
bollocks off.**

FAV: 3,374 RT: 63

The Mrs and I don't have much sex these days, every
few months at best. But we always do on my birthday,
and I usually get more than a quickie. This year a family
friend died a couple of days before and we didn't do it.
So now I'm angry at a dead person.

FAV: 6,956 RT: 82

**I have two kids under eight. They were downstairs
playing, wife joined me in bed, things started getting
good, I was about to put the tip in when both kids
enter the room wailing 'cos they couldn't have a
cuddle with mummy. I wanted to throttle them both.
Fucking cockblockers.**

FAV: 4,531 RT: 52

Husband wonders why our sex life dried up. Dates back
to the Xmas he bought some 'toys' but was most exited
about the hood that covered my whole head except my
mouth. Made me realise he doesn't find me attractive at
all. Binned it. Bought myself a vibrator.

FAV: 10,083 RT: 101

I'm Not a Nonce But...

Remember that time you were still in school and fancying one of the other pupils? Well, they were a child and you are a nonce.

My son gave me an unexpected bear hug from behind and lifted me up and leaned back. I screamed and struggled and in doing so we both fell forward. As we did, his crotch landed up against my backside. We both died a little bit that day and he's never done it since.

FAV: 3,571 RT: 34

> I thanked a man in the acknowledgments of my PhD thesis who was later arrested for child porn. PhD theses end up in the British Library. I'm forever associated with a nonce.
>
> FAV: 4,171 RT: 55

Boss was making a round of layoffs at work. A last throw of the dice, after he verbally fired me, I simply just said, 'I know everything...' Still working there two years later, though I am concerned I'll wind up being innocently arrested for assisting an offender one day.

FAV: 3,881 RT: 51

I once pulled a girl in a night club and went back to hers. Woke up to realise it was my childminder's house and she was the little girl who used to live there. Had to meet the parents in the morning, who totally remembered me from 20 years ago.

FAV: 3,968 RT: 35

I'm Not Gay But...

One of the more regular confession formats is to announce that 'I'm 100 per cent straight but I love cocks' and why not? Everyone can live their lives how they want to. Good for you, you very straight person.

Found my boyfriend's burner phone. Turns out he spends his quiet periods at work meeting other men all over the county to collect rare Pokemon. Phew.

FAV: 20,699 RT: 383

> My wife is so controlling and gets seriously annoyed if I even get a text from a female work colleague, accusing me of all sorts. However, she's happy for me to see my male friends, primarily because she doesn't know I'm fucking one of them.
>
> FAV: 13,348 RT: 289

Wanked a guy off at a nudist beach and got some really positive feedback afterwards. Part of me wants to tell the wife so she knows how great I am at handies.

FAV: 6,413 RT: 100

I'm a straight woman and enjoy watching porn now and again. I'll also watch gay porn. I like seeing two buff guys at it. Gay guys moan and groan, straight guys – maybe it's just Brits – don't make noise during sex. Bores me to tears. So yeah, that's my porn kink. Keep it up, lads.

FAV: 3,317 RT: 40

Back about 30 years ago, I needed somewhere to live. I didn't have a lot of money, so I pretended to be gay and spent six months living with a gay man as his live-in lover. Whenever I visit the city where he still lives, I pop round to see him and we have sex. I feel I must.

FAV: 3,006 RT: 21

Have had a very vanilla monogamous heterosexual sex life for 25 years but last week had a dream I was at a gay orgy and seemed to be having the time of my life. Booked a couple of male escorts the next day and my mind was blown. How do I tell my wife I now prefer cock?

FAV: 3,142 RT: 40

Went through a weird phase in my twenties and had sex with a massive hairy bear of a man. Made me realise I'm not gay, but I regret it because he gave the best cuddles.

FAV: 3,093 RT: 43

I used to sleep with hookers, but now that my wife and I are combining bank accounts I can't pay for them anymore. Now I've had to turn to Grindr and sleep with men instead.

FAV: 3,657 RT: 82

When I was a young teenager I oddly assumed that gay people like anal sex because if someone came in your ass, you'd get this awesome anal orgasm. So I wanked and poured my cum into a little plastic water pistol and fired it up my my ass. Didn't get any kind of anal orgasm.

FAV: 6,338 RT: 116

I Blew a Definite Shag

It's quite normal to wake up at 5 in the morning and realise that someone 20 years ago was flirting with you and you screwed it up because you're a massive dork.

As a teen, an attractive girl knocked on my door with her friend and asked me out but I declined as there was a bloke doing Meatloaf on *Stars in Their Eyes* from my home town, Oldham, and I didn't want to miss it. He didn't win and she never asked again.

Sorry Sir, Our Brains Have Been Rotted by Pornography, Delicious Pornography

----

There have been absolutely no consequences for society that everyone is walking around with machines that instantly display every obscenity you can imagine by saying 'Google, show me naughty pics' in their pockets.

I made the error of saying out loud, in front of my wife and daughter, that the clock on the ITV coverage of the World Cup is very similar to the Pornhub colour scheme and style. Cover blown.

**When someone posts
a picture of their bath
on social media, I take the
time to study the image for
reflections on the taps.**

My wife decided that we should watch porn together for the first time. I had to Google 'porn' and pretend I didn't know what I was doing.

Having married a woman with big boobs, whenever I'm looking at porn and see a big-boobed woman I can't help thinking, 'Oh, I bet she has back problems.'

Sex Boasts

If there's one thing people like more than sex, it's telling people they've had sex so that they can feel smug.

I was with my boyfriend for 9 years. Every October I would change my groans in bed to 'ooohhh' like a ghost, climaxing in an appropriate way for Halloween. We thought it was funny but I did this on Saturday with my new partner and, pardon the pun, he's ghosted me.

On a camping holiday with my ex, one night the tent next to us started having loud sex. Ex got horny and we started too, basically an orgy but in separate tents. Best sex I've ever had.

I'm having an affair with a woman from work and one of the reasons I was so attracted to her was her flawless use of spelling, punctuation and grammar in work emails. There is nothing sexier than a woman who uses an Oxford comma.

Halfway through pulling the hottest girl I've ever met, too much booze meant I went to the toilet to be sick. I didn't want to smell like sick so my only option was to crunch up a couple of urinal cakes. I told her the odd taste was a shot I'd just done at the bar and it worked.

While working on viral marketing for a popular sci-fi franchise, I needed to quickly model an alien with a wrinkly skin texture. In a fit of chaotic energy, I 3D-scanned my ballsack and used that. Every so often I remember that almost a million people have seen my balls.

I'm currently seeing a brunette, a blonde and a redhead. My house has never been so clean with all the vacuuming I'm doing.

Went to a stranger's house for a Tinder hookup. He was delighted when I turned up without my knickers on under my dress. I didn't tell him I'd had to take off the tight shapewear bottoms I had been wearing because they were making me fart with every exhale.

When me and my girlfriend have sex doggy-style I sometime pull on her bra straps and pretend I'm on a dog sled. Kinda turns me on too.

Got a blow job from a girl at uni, asked her if she could tell a few people I have a massive cock. Unbelievably she did and I'm now known for it. Have to piss in cubicles to avoid getting found out.

I Do Right by My Closeted Father

Gad Dad was everyone's favourite pop group in Britpop, right? And rightly so, here's a big thumbs up for all the gay mums and dads.

My old dad – divorced from my mum – lives in an old people's home. His 'son-in-law' visits his room every 2 weeks or so to say hi. In reality he's a bloke we found on Grindr who's into older guys and gives Dad a good time. No regrets. Care home doesn't know.

While scrolling through photos on my dad's phone at a family wedding, I stumbled on pictures of him being fucked up the arse by another man with an elastic band around his cock. I've never said anything to him about it.

Recently my dad was showing me pictures of where he'd been working, which was all very impressive until the next picture was him with a hard-on on the bed. He said 'oops' and that was that.

FAV: 3,751 RT: 67

Your Guide to Men Having a Wank

Apparently men never stop playing with it. Who knew?

My wife works nights. She thinks I sit at home and wank. I don't. I stream myself playing Farming Simulator online. I prefer her thinking I wank.

FAV: 5,404 RT: 88

Was having a quick wank and I heard my wife coming up the stairs, panicked, hid my iPad just before she walked in but still had my cock in my hand. She looked at me, then looked at the TV, making me to also look. To my horror, *Loose Women* was on. She thinks I wank over daytime TV.

FAV: 5,198 RT: 87

Wife and kids went out so decided to have a wank in the living room. Did not want to shoot on carpet so waddled over and shot into the sawdust inside my kid's pet guinea pig cage. Unsure if related but guinea pig died about a week later. God bless you, Patches

FAV: 5,307 RT: 128

When I was a horny teen I thought I'd gamed the system by never calling sex lines for more than 60 seconds because they were all charged by the minute. When the family phone bill came through I realised how wrong I was.

FAV: 3,276 RT: 37

My mate's wife has a great pair boobs and I frequently enjoy her holiday bikini pics. Ibiza 2019 is a fav. I crop my mate out, though, I'm not an animal.

FAV: 5,494 RT: 65

My spreadsheet of wanks and sexual conquests goes back 40 years to when I was 17. I transferred it all to Excel a few years back and colour-coded everything. It's a work of art.

FAV: 4,304 RT: 72

My wife has put cameras around the house to check up on our dogs when we go out. When I'm home alone, finding a place to knock one out requires special-forces-level planning.

FAV: 4,544 RT: 69

As a porn-obsessed teen I wondered what it felt like to get a facial so one day when wanking on my bed, I put my feet up above my head and came on my own face. It went straight in my eye and I ended up getting conjunctivitis.

FAV: 5,202 RT: 87

**Every Saturday morning
the guy next door goes fishing.
His wife plays ABBA
and audibly masturbates,
it's the highlight of my week.**

My best mate is a joiner. In my house I have a really creaky stair which he keeps promising to fix. I don't want it fixed and never pursue it. It's my wanking stair – my 10 second early warning system if my partner comes downstairs and I'm mid-wank.

FAV: 3,032 RT: 34

Married and been together for many years. We have a healthy sex life, however since following Fesshole I'm scared to leave the house too often in case my husband wanks himself to death.

FAV: 6,769 RT: 88

Women Wank Too

We know what you're doing ladies, buying AA batteries from the petrol station at 3am. In the words of David A Stewart of the Eurythmics, 'Sisters Are Doing It For Themselves'.

I told my husband I wasn't in the mood for sex. It was because I had injured my clitoris with my vibrator earlier in the day.

FAV: 6,225 RT: 74

Whenever we have Sunday morning sex, I ask my husband to run a bath afterwards. That's so while he gets in the bath I can have a wank and finish off properly.

FAV: 3,296 RT: 25

HAVE YOUR SAY

~~~~~~

If you're stuck for a reply to a fess and want some examples that are more original than 'Kitchen sofa?!', then learn from these fine people:

Ended up back at a girl's house after a night out. She said she wanted to make me cum with her mouth. She then proceeded to literally suck me off like she could draw the jizz out of my cock like it's a straw. Left me with a love bite on my bellend. She was 28. Why had nobody told her?

Maybe she saved the best fellator?

The wife of one of my best friends has been sending me naked pictures of her for nearly 2 years. Have about 20 now. I have never acknowledged them, replied or spoken to her about it, as I don't know if she thinks she's sending them to someone else and I don't want her to stop.

I once sent a naked photo to everybody in my address book. Not only was it embarrassing, but it cost me a fortune in stamps.

I matched a girl on Tinder on a Tuesday evening. She asked
if she was OK to bring a change of clothes etc as she had
work the next day. I woke in the morning and found her sat on
my sofa tapping away on her laptop with a headset on.
'I'm choosing to work from home today,' she said.

**She sounds like a keeper.
Mainly cause it
doesn't sound like
you have a choice.**

I once put on a wig and fake tattoos to make a sex tape
with a guy off Tinder. It has more than 4 million views and
my husband has no clue that it's me in it.

**If he finds out,
there'll be hell
toupee...**

Thou Shalt Have Largely Negative Feelings About Work

Nobody wants to work.

Hopefully reading this section

will make you throw off the chains of

capitalism so we all can live in

paradise where we do fuck all except

shag and laugh at jokes.

Having been in four disciplinaries at work, I can confirm that nothing scares an HR department like a call pretending to be a lawyer representing the member of staff.

A group of us have a deal in work. When one of us wants to go do something, we start an audio-only Teams meeting with someone. We play white noise and the other person either goes out as well or puts headphones on. If the recording is pulled, it just sounds corrupted.

I've been a yoga instructor for over 20 years. I've instructed a few celebrities. I started at 14 so I could suck my own knob. Eight weeks of training to realise I don't like dick in my mouth. Still, it set me up for life.

I Fucked Up at Work

Our biggest work fuck up was while working at an environment charity, responding to someone who'd written in going, 'What are you going to do about the whales?' Thinking we were just joking to our boss and not replying to them directly, we wrote: 'Eat them – the white meat of the sea.' Oops.

Designer for a well-known brand. All our men's shoes were a size bigger than other standard sizes for a season because I fucked up the spreadsheet with the measurements.

As a junior doctor in casualty I once closed a cut on a lad's scrotum with wound glue – he'd injured himself climbing over a railing. As he got up he screamed. It turned out I'd glued his balls to his leg.

FAV: 6,306 RT: 154

I once worked as a psych nurse in a special hospital. Lost the med room keys one day and locked the whole hospital down while everywhere was searched. Three hours later, we were 10 minutes away from a full lock change which would've cost £600k when I found them in my back pocket.

FAV: 5,643 RT: 83

I lied about speaking French on my CV for a job and got away with it for a few weeks using Google Translate and emails until I had to take a phone call in front of my boss and couldn't read out the translations quickly enough.

FAV: 3,318 RT: 56

I Hate My Colleague

The horror that is colleagues, your enforced daylight family whom you can't divorce.

A woman I work with has left the job twice and returned twice. Every time she's left, there's been a collection and I've contributed. I'm pretty sure no one says it, but we all want our money back.

FAV: 6,510 RT: 93

There's a bloke at work who doesn't eat any veg or fruit. After 20 years sharing an office, I can recognise him in the next cubicle by the smell and the horrendous wet flapping sound his sphincter makes.

I'm the cheery guy in our office WhatsApp group who sends happy motivational memes of encouragement and joyful emojis. I do it because in a recent leadership assessment, I got told I need to create more trust in my team. In reality, I hate the bastards and wish they'd all die.

Petty Revenge on People I Work With

The quickest way to alienate a colleague is to start marking their emails out of 10.

My gaffer is a twat. In a cost-cutting exercise he sent an email to the entire company complaining that company-provided milk was only for tea/coffee and NOT for cornflakes. I forwarded the email to a national newspaper who published it with the headline 'CEREAL OFFENDERS'.

When we left our IT job we hid a server below the floor panels, connected and powered. They'll be searching for years for the location of that machine.

I used to open the printer drawer, take a out a good inch or so of paper, then draw a spunking cock on the top sheet. I'd then replace the paper back in the printer drawer and, eventually, somebody would end up with a spunking cock on an email or report they'd printed.

FAV: 3,188 RT: 50

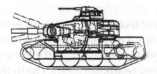

A guy at work once accidentally typed 'Many tanks' instead of 'Many thanks' at the end of an email. Ever since I've made an effort to end every email to him with 'Many tanks' and copy at least 3 pics of tanks. I'm genuinely scared that I'm going to run out of tank pics on Google.

FAV: 4,917 RT: 107

I'm an in-house photographer for a large org. Every board member has a headshot on the wall with their heads about 10 per cent too big. Never told a soul but I smile as I walk through reception every day. Never gets old.

FAV: 4,266 RT: 54

I sat opposite a miserable woman, Jane, who made everyone around her uncomfortable. A few times a week I would get Microsoft text speak to say 'Jane' at a low volume. From her reaction you knew she could hear it but didn't know where it was coming from. She ended up moving desks.

FAV: 3,932 RT: 47

I Did Crime with the Office Resources

Come the apocalypse, they who stole fifteen hole punches will inherit the Earth.

I left my old job over two years ago. I never gave my work mobile back and nobody noticed. It still hasn't been switched off. Occasionally when drunk I send a text and adopt a snow leopard for a tenner a go. I now have adopted enough leopards to populate a small zoo.

FAV: 7,892 RT: 114

We aren't allowed to use the milk at work because it's 'company stock' and are told we have to bring in our own and label it. Every Saturday morning I walk straight into the kitchen, grab a fresh bottle from delivery and label it as staff milk.

FAV: 3,234 RT: 31

When working in a local Co-Op, I used to take any limited edition 50p coins from the tills and sell them on eBay. I then used the money earned from this to buy my first car. Justice for the minimum wage they paid me.

FAV: 5,897 RT: 63

I left a large company and clicked 'download all contacts' in the CRM system. Surprisingly I got 120k email addresses which I took to my new job at a start-up company. I sent an introductory email to them all and made £1m sales and £50k commission in the first week.

Once worked for a company who tried using incentives for good reviews. If a customer mentioned you by name on the site you'd get £10. I not only left lots of fake reviews for myself but to avoid suspicion did the same for my colleagues. Racked up hundreds of pounds before leaving.

How to Save Money at Work

If you don't steal pens and pencils from the office, are you really an employee?

I have 3 large battery power banks that I charge at work during my mandatory 1 day in the office. I use them to power all my devices for the rest of the week. Every little helps.

I'm in charge of buying at my company. I'm supposed to find the cheapest price for all products, but instead I always choose companies that are on TopCashBack and buy through my account. I make approximately £1500 a year for myself, but it costs the company about £15k.

I Abuse My Position of Power Quite Mildly to Amuse Myself

Just some people who are messing up the system from within, but not very much, and good for them.

I am the finance controllor for my organisation. The admin team order Tetley teabags and are confused every time when Yorkshire arrive. Little do they know, I amend the PO and remove Tetleys and replace it with Yorkshire. I will not drink that piss water.

FAV: 17,254 RT: 387

I work in a chip shop and always ask customers if they want vinegar and salt.

FAV: 4,078 RT: 65

When I worked in a shop, I used to keep aside the 'Smoking harms your unborn child' fag packets to sell to our visibly pregnant customers.

FAV: 3,721 RT: 28

I work for a children's publishing company who chronically underpay their staff, so to protest, I hide very, very faint images of cocks in each picture book until they fire me. It's been four years and the ghostly cocks are still going strong.

FAV: 4,944 RT: 143

I Abuse My Position of Power for Good

Small heroes working from inside the machine.

Part of my job in a hospital is to book appointments for patients via text message. I deliberately give people from affluent areas really early ones so they have to deal with rush hour and an early morning. The working classes get a lie-in.

FAV: 13,452 RT: 295

I work for an online supermarket and to help out older customers I always put 100 returned bags through on their order even if they don't give me any. They get 10p per bag so £10 off their shopping. The company made £70m profit last year, so they won't miss it.

FAV: 18,682 RT: 284

As a doctor, I know that a lot of my patients' ailments are in the mind. They are lonely. I arrange appointments to 'match-make' those who I think will get on. I keep them waiting so they have chance to 'meet' in the waiting room. Twenty years and six marriages. Call me Cilla.

FAV: 22,890 RT: 451

I work in a school and the caretaker gave me the code for the bell in my building so I could ring it to signify the two minute silence for The Queen. I then used it to reprogram the timings and now the last bell on Friday rings three minutes early.

FAV: 4,589 RT: 41

I work at McDonald's. After accidentally while hungover giving someone more chicken nuggets than I should have and seeing how happy that made them I try to add extra items in orders now. I love seeing the look happiness from something so small and insignificant.

I Abuse My Position of Power Terribly

Small Hitlers who are fucking with you for their lols. Be careful out there.

I work in customs at Gatwick airport. My favourite thing to do is to spot engagement rings in a passenger's luggage. I then pull out said ring as part of a 'routine check' spoiling the surprise for the unsuspecting partner. Yes, I'm a troubled soul.

I was chair of an interview panel and didn't give the best candidate the job because they were too fucking cheerful and I couldn't put up with that shit every day.

I work in police custody. If we get a particularly cunty prisoner in, I like to turn on the torch on their phone to run its battery down. This way they can't use their phone when we eventually kick them out.

My job thinks I am working
from home in Milton Keynes
but actually I moved to Greece
six months ago and log in
every day via VPN.

FAV: 21,770 RT: 451

I'm a director of a firm with 220 employees. I've made redundancies specifically targeting people unable to accept that Secret Santa should be kept secret and instead interrogate everyone involved. Mentally fragile control freaks. Not regretted losing any of them.

I work in HR. When I interview I always start the meeting with 'Hello there.' If the candidate responds with 'General Kenobi' they get the job, no matter what. I have hired three people who were useless purely based on this.

I Am Destroying the Business from Within

Are you bored at work? Why not be the grit in the machine, the shit in the coffee or just phone in a bomb threat?

I am a mid-level civil servant and work from home. I work very hard and love my job. Each time an MP implies people who WFH are lazy, I send an email full of faux outrage about a local issue to their local newspaper. Six have been published and two have had a response from the MP.

Someone keeps grassing up the company I work for over bad practices, bad hygiene etc, causing loss of sales and bad relationships with customers. It's me. I hate the shithole.

At work I'm a real proper goody twos-shoes and everyone knows it. I put in an anonymous fake complaint to HR about myself doing drugs, swearing and being abusive to staff. Got three weeks paid at home while the company eventually got around to investigating and clearing me.

FAV: 13,303 RT: 250

I work for a government department. I often submit FOI requests using an anonymous website in the hope that a someone will pick up on a story about how corrupt this government is.

FAV: 7,557 RT: 561

The multimillion-pound business I work for has suggested staff cut open shampoo bottles and use every last drop to save money rather than give us a pay rise. I just accidentally switched off their billing system for eight hours. The panic is real.

FAV: 16,170 RT: 26

How to Succeed in Job Interviews

Our genuine tip for job interviews is to try and show empathy for the person interviewing – they are going to have to work with you and as much as they want someone useful, they want someone who might be nice to them, because it's lonely being the boss.

I never finished university. Nobody knows this – not my wife, friends or employer. They all think that degree is real. In fact, I made it myself on my computer, in MS Paint.

FAV: 14,375 RT: 211

I was being interviewed for a job and the receptionist asked if I wanted tea or coffee. I was so nervous, I just answered 'Yes please.' Five minutes later she brought me in both a tea and a coffee and I had to sit through the interview like a psychopath alternating between both cups.

I was once put on the spot in a job interview with the question 'How would your best friend describe you?' Nerves took over and my natural defenses kicked in. What came out of my mouth was, 'Well, he'd probably say I'm a bit of a cunt.'

I Procastinate and Skive at Work

You shouldn't worry about your imposter syndrome – these people don't.

I regularly book fake meetings with work friends where we basically spend an hour chatting.

My Football Manager addiction has reached a point where I may require professional help. Today, I accidently shared a five page PowerPoint on a list of potential signings for my RB Leipzig game with a client. Her response was, 'My teenage son loves that game!' I'm 47 years old.

I work for a water company. It's double pay on Sundays so I regularly call in ghost jobs with a funny voice to give myself work for then. I sit in my van and watch YouTube all day.

I asked ChatGPT to help me write a business case I've struggled with for weeks. It failed miserably, clearly getting every detail wrong. Happy to know machines can't replace me yet, but also terrified now the deadline's today and I've wasted all my time talking to a robot.

I Don't Know How to Do My Job

You don't need to know anything to work anywhere – just google it. Fake it until you make it.

I have been working as a press photographer for fifteen years. I have no idea how to use a camera. I put it in automatic mode and hope for the best. I've won two national awards from Press Associations with photos I got lucky with. I've made a great living from something I can't do.

I have no idea what my job is, I just respond positively to emails and say to anyone copied in, 'You should be able to get that sorted, right ?' They even promoted me and I asked what's involved. 'Just keep doing what you're doing for more pay.'

I'm the head of IT for a multi-billion-dollar corporation. I get my wife to do Excel formulae and charts as I have no idea.

I was weeding the front garden and a passing old lady asked me if I was a gardener. I was bored in retirement so said yes, now I'm looking after her garden and a number of her friends. I have fuck all clue what I'm doing. Anything beyond weeding and mowing is down to Google.

I'm a reasonably well-known chef in a popular restaurant in my city with 20 years experience but I have no idea what onions & garlic add to most dishes. I just put them in because everyone else does.

Fuck Clients

Clients and customers are all arseholes. Here's how to deal with the worst ones.

I run a small business and work on a daily rate. When a client is late paying I add a day's work to their next invoice for every week they're late. Last month I earned an extra £2.5k.

I'm a postie. If an address just has a house name instead of a number I purposely work out the house number, knock on and ask for example, 'Number 26?' It drives the pretentious assholes insane.

Be Nice to the Staff or Else

You know that person who serves you in Costa? Just be polite – it costs you nothing, and prevents them from spitting in your extra-frothy espresso.

I'm an electrician. Offer me a cup of tea, job gets done for the quoted price. Don't offer, I'm always going to find an 'unforeseen problem' that costs extra. I don't care about the tea, but it's a good indicator of people's attitude to the working class.

I work on social media for a top UK supermarket. Sometimes after work I'll log into my troll account and abuse the customers that are cunts since I can't do it on the work account.

I'm a photographer. If someone at the event I'm photographing is rude to me or comes across as a bit of a prick, I make sure in my edits that I make the pictures as unflattering as possible. I had a rude grandma before, so I sharpened all her wrinkles and added a few extra chins.

I work in retail and keep a security tag in my pocket. If I see a customer being rude to staff, I swing my hip near the detector as they leave, so they have to tip out their bags to prove they're not shoplifters. If they moan, I do it again. Petty, but satisfying.

When I worked in Greggs, if you were rude I'd either squeeze the tongs really hard to disfigure your pastry or give you as much change as possible so you had loads of pointless pennies. If you were a dick, both. I'm already forced to wear a stupid hat, don't make my day worse.

Plumber by trade. Once worked in a bloke's house, he was sat doing a 5,000-piece puzzle on the table. After his constant moaning, I decided to pocket a piece as I was leaving . The pleasure I got knowing he would never complete it still brings me joy 12 years on.

I'm a pharmacist. If you're rude to me or I don't like you, you are getting a 28-pack of tablets made up of cut-up foils containing one and two tablets each.

Tradesmen's Secrets

This is the insider shit that'll give you the skinny on how things really work inside Britain.

I'm an airline pilot. Sometimes we put the seatbelt signs on just so there's no line for the bathroom when we go out. Sorry not sorry.

FAV: 18,818 RT: 351

I'm a postman. When you order something from Ann Summers we all know. The label on the parcel says 'Gold Group International' which is the holding company. We know you've been ordering your kinky underwear and sex toys.

FAV: 15,526 RT: 369

Bricklayer here. Can't remember why this started but every new build I've done I've done a shit down the gap between the breeze blocks and the outer bricks. 500+ houses in Liverpool got shits in them.

FAV: 14,258 RT: 438

Carpet fitter here. If I refuse a cup of tea from you with the excuse 'Just had one on the last job', it's because you are a manky bastard and I don't trust your hygiene.

FAV: 7,935 RT: 142

I'm a bathroom fitter. Most clients, mostly men, make a joke about being the first to use 'the throne'. Let me tell you now, they never ever are.

FAV: 2,996 RT: 37

I'm a postman and if you have a low letterbox
there's a 90 per cent chance your post is
going through a neighbour's door with a
higher letterbox or just not getting delivered.
Fuck anyone with a low letterbox.

I was a taxi driver for a while and the whole 'fake taxi' thing is rubbish. However I now work for a debt collection agency and the number of women that offer themselves to pay the debt is surprising. Never taken them up on the offers as the can of worms it could open is crazy.

I'm a mastering engineer. When bands send me shit songs to master, all I do is pass it through a basic audio plugin to make it sound louder. Had no complaints. No point wasting time on polishing a turd.

My wife and I use a sugar baby site. We use it to get guys to pay her for talking to them. They don't know it's usually me talking to them as she's too busy working and I work from home. It's amazing how much money guys throw out to a hot girl just for talking and pics.

Anybody working in HR who says they do it cause they love people is a liar. We do it cause we're nosey bastards and love sacking shitcunts.

Teachers Tell All

Here's today's lesson from the teaching professions: they need to be paid better to deal with your smelly kids.

Teacher here. If you give your child's teacher smellies, candles or anything akin to bubble bath/ soaps at the end of term, they will all end up in the tombola at the next school fête. We really only love wine and Prosecco, thanks.

I'm a teacher. People who moan about the lengthy holidays we get always have children who are little shits. I don't blame them, I wouldn't want to spend six weeks trapped with their vile spawn either.

Teacher here. Got called a wanker by a 15-year-old in my class. When I wrote his end-of-year report, I made sure the first letter of the first word of each sentence spelled out WANKER. It was checked. It went home. Best moment in teaching.

I'm a headteacher. My head of music recently released an album of his own music. It's not my cup of tea but I keep it on repeat on Spotify because I love that he hasn't given up on his dreams.

I work at a school and had the
job of putting a time capsule
together to celebrate the
diamond jubilee. After the
well-attended burial ceremony
I found I'd forgot to put any of
the items in the capsule.
I've never told anyone.
I think of the empty capsule
at least three times a day.

FAV:10,233 RT:181

I'm a chemistry teacher. Since the start of the year, somebody's been pilfering the snacks I keep in my desk. They're about to learn the most important chemistry lesson of all: phenolphthalein indicator is also a powerful laxative.

Public Transport

To do an office job you have to get there, so let's celebrate the public transport workers that make this happen.

Bus driver here. In traffic, I play a game where I lock eyes with dogs in the boots of cars. They either look away and I win, or they go absolutely apeshit and start jumping about and I still win.

I'm a bus driver. If I see you get in trying to sneak on with glasses of alcohol etc I won't stop you. I like to play a game of 'How many potholes can I hit on the journey?' and 'Who can I make wear most of their drink?' Beep-beep.

I'm a tube driver on the London Underground and I get such a great satisfaction from closing the doors on people and splitting up their groups. I don't do it to young children with parents, but anyone else is fine.

**Train driver here. Whenever
I see someone waving goodbye
to a partner/family member/
friend from the platform to the
train, I hold the train for a minute
or so, just long enough to make
the waving become awkward.**

FAV: 16,088 RT: 412

HAVE YOUR SAY

Good replies to Fesshole fessions that aren't people posting a photo of John Peel and saying, 'Coming up next it's Good Replies to Fesshole Fessions with their track "A Photo of John Peel"'

Boss just sent me home from work and told me to take as much time as I need, no questions asked, after a colleague found me at my desk with tears streaming down my face and unable to talk. Truth is, I'd pulled a hair out of my nose and it was fucking agony.

You can sue for a depilating workplace injury

I work for a large consultancy. When we hire new graduates I have a filter set up to automatically reject anyone who uses 'could of' anywhere in their application. I've rejected hundreds this way.

This could of course cause false positives

Nothing quite ruins fancying someone at work like working in HR. Just found out from a sick note that the pretty girl I've fancied for six months has piles. Put me right off.

Creep from HR has been giving me the eye, so I got my doctor to write a sick note saying I have piles

I work nights in IT support with my girlfriend. One night we had sex to pass the boredom. As I came, I pulled out and shot my load onto a server rack, which stopped working. Several trading firms called in to say their platforms stoped working. Cost them £23m in lost trades.

Least plausible bit of this is someone in IT support having sex

Thou Shalt Love Your Home Life (and House)

Living in your own home is hard.

All that council tax and

taking the bins out – it's like

a terrible RPG that you can't win

as there's always another meal to plan.

I always buy meals for two at the supermarket because I don't want people to think I'm a sad loner. But then I eat them and wonder why I'm a fat bastard.

I've been with my wife for nearly 20 years and once we had dinner around 5pm and we both thought we were hungry at 10pm and ordered a curry and I long for it to happen again.

My wife throws away any food past its use by date on the dot. I try and make a point of eating it to prove her wrong and that the date is just a guide. The salmon I ate yesterday has proved her right and me horrifically wrong. I was proved wrong over and over and over again.

Cooking at Home

Imagine we're Jamie Oliver – that is, someone who's going to take away your Turkey Twizzlers and demand that you eat healthily, like this:

I carry two cooked sausages in a poo bag when I take the dog out. When the dog takes a crap I pretend to pick it up but never do. Never have. Anyone says anything and I point to the bag pretending it's poo. After walkies, me and the dog have a sausage each.

I once peeled off hard dead skin from my feet and simmered it in the frying pan. It tastes exactly like the skin of cooked rotisserie chicken. I'd never do it again, but wanted to try.

FAV: 3,413 RT: 102

> **I regularly serve a bowl of Dreamies cat treats among other buffet food at parties. No one notices and they are all gone at the end of the night.**
>
> FAV: 4,617 RT: 201

Ate three raw pork sausages to avoid a dinner party. Didn't get ill and turns out I love the taste. Now I spread it on toast like it's pâté, not been ill once.

FAV: 7,616 RT: 116

A coffee snob friend was visiting imminently and we were out of milk. I had some Sainsbury's cat milk in the fridge. I tasted a bit and thought, fuck it, that'll do. He complimented me on how delightfully creamy the coffee was.

FAV: 5,401 RT: 81

My girlfriend and I have started using strawberry flavoured lube while having sex and I have become very accustomed to the taste. So much so that when she isn't around I'll spread some on my toast if we don't have jam.

FAV: 5,384 RT: 138

Bins

The only thing that unites Britain is a hatred of Duran Duran's third LP and the shout 'WHEN IS BINS?'

My neighbour keeps using my wheelie bin so that he doesn't have to wheel his out to the pavement. I've padlocked mine shut and only open it on collection day. I take great pleasure watching him having to take his bin out now. It's the small victories in life.

If you can't be arsed to drag your wheelie bin back in off the street within 24 hours of it being emptied, you deserve whatever ends up in there. That includes the content of my cat's litter tray, you lazy fucks.

How to Save Money at Home

The best tip for saving money at home is to move somewhere cheaper, like back to your mum's.

The flat underneath mine is empty and has been for a while. I arranged a viewing so I could up the thermostat when the letting agent wasn't looking to save on me putting my heating on so much.

Nice bloke in the flat above who I get along with has incredibly fast and expensive internet. Password is exactly what's written on the bottom of the router. Took note of it while in his place for a beer a few years back and cancelled my own package. Still works.

FAV: 10,698 RT: 87

> **I've been asking my boyfriend to join me in the shower recently. Poor fucker thinks I can't resist him. The truth is it's saving us nearly £10 a week in electricity.**
>
> FAV: 13,868 RT: 265

I've not paid the £28 annual fee for garden waste this year. Every fortnight we ride the gauntlet of bin collection day. My guilt-ridden angst of being found out dissipates as another bin is collected. Oh the euphoria of getting one over the Tory bastards that run the council!

FAV: 3,933 RT: 38

My neighbour has said the energy bill crisis is just media scaremongering and people these days are too soft. Our houses share a single loft with no wall between them, so while he's on holiday I've popped up and swapped his insulation round for my cheaper stuff.

FAV: 3,288 RT: 47

Girlfriend likes us to get the expensive clothes washing powder/liquid, as 'it smells nicer and makes the clothes softer'. Darling, the washing powder ran out two weeks ago and I've been using three drops of Fairy Liquid. No complaints yet.

FAV: 3,024 RT: 34

I was lying down in the park
once in a work lunch hour.
A bird shat in my mouth.
I assume it was a pigeon who
had recently eaten a plum as it
tasted vaguely fruity.
I spat it out discreetly and
never told a soul.

Revenge on Neighbours

Here's some people you wouldn't want to live next door to.

I rang the police anonymously on my neighbours, saying I'd buried a dead body in the back garden 20 years ago. This was after a full garden landscape they had done. Watched from an upstairs window as the police dug it all up.

FAV: 5,202 RT: 172

My neighbour is a massive cunt. I've had a number of run-ins with him, but his cat is lovely and spends most of his time at my house. The amount of satisfaction I get from thinking even his own cat thinks he's a cunt is huge.

FAV: 7,502 RT: 138

One day I overheard my neighbours calling my dog ugly. So now whenever they are trying to enjoy a peaceful evening in the garden, I give my dog his squeakiest toys to play with so it ruins their night. My dog is a very good boy.

FAV: 11,901 RT: 196

My postie dropped a bunch of blank 'Sorry we missed you' cards in my building's foyer. For the last three months my neighbours have been sent on missions to retrieve non-existent parcels from the post office depending on how loud they are, or how much their dog barks.

FAV: 6,510 RT: 187

I write Happy Holidays in the Christmas cards of our *Daily Mail*-reading neighbours knowing it will annoy the fuck out of them.

My former neighbours came straight from hell. Partying 3–4 times a week, with a lot of booze and drugs. Their oldest son was dealing drugs as well. We couldn't take it anymore and put the house up for sale. There were multiple people interested, we chose the policeman.

Neighbour used to boast about living with her fella and not claiming together, therefore claiming benefits she wasn't entitled to. Changed wi-fi name to DWP Surveillance, she noticed it, shat it and updated her claim.

We had an extension built. It was unfinished and our neighbour took photos of our garden and put them on Facebook saying how horrible it was. We rendered the whole extension apart from the wall that faces her window, so now she has to look at bare breezeblocks whenever she looks outside.

I live on the end of a terrace, my next-door neighbour is one miserable cunt. It's –6°C outside, so I decided to turn all the radiators off on the party wall. Why should I pay to warm his bricks up as well as mine? I'd rather suffer than make him comfortable.

My neighbour is so anal about parking her car right outside her house, to the extent that she will go out and move the car 10 yards just so it is perfectly positioned. I make a point of parking in that spot whenever it is free, even if there is space outside my own house.

FAV: 5,783 RT: 39

Revenge on Flatmates

The trick to getting along with your flatmates is to live alone.

I was at uni in halls. Stuff always being stolen from our fridge. I bought a carton of UHT milk, wrote 'Do not use', then added an 'ingredient' from the photo lab. Next day it was gone. Dude upstairs literally shat himself unconscious, ended up in hospital on a drip. Oops.

FAV: 7,067 RT: 106

I turned the toaster volume up to max on my housemates after an argument so they'd burn their toast in the morning.

FAV: 8,185 RT: 117

My housemates would always steal my food and abuse my stuff at uni, so as the head tenant, I photoshopped all of our bills to be more expensive, so they all covered my share of the real bill. Didn't pay a penny towards utilities for two years.

FAV: 7,353 RT: 92

Living in student halls, a guy would always come home from the pub and jump up on one of the bollards outside and shout something incoherent, waking everyone up. One night I smeared Vaseline on all of the bollards. Broke his wrist when he fell, but it never happened again.

My pot-smoking housemate used to leave the back door open to get rid of the smell of his weed. It's freezing and heating isn't cheap so I sold the TV and told my landlord that someone walked in the open door and stole it. He got evicted, I got £300, a brand new TV and cheaper bills.

Landlords Are Going to Be First Against the Wall in the Glorious Revolution

----

There's a lot of anger about landlords in Britain and this is largely because they're all wankers.

Moved into a flat with sash windows with no locks. Landlord promised to pay me back if I fitted some myself, which I did – good ones too – and then he never paid me. When I moved out, I clicked them locked and took the keys with me.

I work in a well-known hardware shop. If I realise that you're a landlord, we don't have the cheap item in stock and you're buying the higher-quality version. It's the only up-selling I do.

I pay my arsehole landlord a fixed monthly fee for water. He sent the plumber round yesterday to look for a leak because his bill was high. Little does he know I leave the shower on while I go to work for 8 hours.

I Love My Cat

Adding a cat to a house is what makes it a home. And smell of old lady piss

My wife wouldn't let me get a cat. So I adopted one from the Cats Protection and pretended like it was a local stray that kept coming to our house and persuaded us to take her in. We've had her 4 years today.

Vet sent a postcard reminder for our cat 'Hunny' to have her annual check-up. I phoned them and asked them to change it to 'Honey'. I was fucking fuming. Never told the cat.

**I have several cats,
and sometimes I pretend
to have a heart attack
and collapse in a heap
on the floor, motionless,
to see how they'd react.
They don't give a fuck.
Ever.**

FAV: 19,067 RT: 636

Cats Are Weird Little Guys but the Best

If you haven't lived with a pet, you're missing out. They're like the furry children it's legal to get castrated.

We had a cappuccino machine. I thought my wife kept cleaning the crispy dried milk off the steamer spout, she thought I was doing it. A year later, after coffee every morning, we found out the cat was licking it off when we were at work.

FAV: 18,474 RT: 584

After two years of cat ownership, I have just started saying 'Oooo, big stretch' when I stretch as well.

FAV: 4,319 RT: 94

Whenever I pick up my cat, I kiss him on the head before I put him down. He now bows his head for a kiss to let me know he WANTS to be put down, and even just when he wants to leave my lap. He clearly thinks it's mandatory and I haven't set him straight.

FAV: 9,101 RT: 162

Dogs, You Love Them

The people of Britain love dogs. You have submitted more canine material to Fesshole than about your own kids.

Visiting friends with my wife, and their dog took a particular interest in me, just sat in front of me wagging its tail. Turned out it was a retired sniffer dog and unknown to everyone else I had a gram of coke in my pocket.

FAV: 17,293 RT: 325

I'm a tradesman and if you have a cute dog, when I come in your house there is 100 per cent chance I'm gonna stroke it for what is probably an uncomfortable length of time for everyone. Best part of the job.

FAV: 5,647 RT: 61

Dogs Are Kinda Grim Too, Actually

Let's be honest, animals that sniff each other's butts and eat shit can be problematic. But hey, don't knock butt-sniffing until you've huffed a few anal vapours.

My wife caught me squatting over the dog, holding its nose directly against my arsehole while I farted straight into its nostrils. No words were spoken but I feel it might be the beginning of the end.

FAV: 6,665 RT: 212

When toilet training my toddler, he did a poo in his potty but a bit went on his shorts. I took him upstairs to clean him up, and came back down to a clean, pristine potty. That's odd, I thought, until I saw my dog looking guilty and licking her lips. This is my dog's confession.

FAV: 5,851 RT: 77

My dog follows me to the bathroom when I go to the toilet. After I wipe, sometimes I let him sniff the tissue before it goes in the bowl. It's my way of saying thank you for the company. He always gives a little wag when I do.

FAV: 3,452 RT: 64

The Unexpected Benefits and Joys of Dog Ownership

Dogs are great. They're always pleased to see you, just like the taxman.

After a heavy drinking session, I shat the bed. Told the wife it was the dog to avoid embarrassment. The size and stench were so bad that she took him to the vet and found out he was showing early signs of stomach cancer. I inadvertently saved my dog but can never take credit.

FAV: 32,075 RT: 819

I've had diarrhea for three years and never saw a doctor. My dog had diarrhea for seven days and I took him to the vet. He has a wheat allergy. I decided to see a doctor and I also have a wheat allergy. We both poo normally now.

FAV: 50,841 RT: 1,231

My dog accidenally ate a bit of weed butter. He got pretty stoned so I joined him. Had a great chat and I introduced him to classic rock music.

Got caught cheating only because the dog was growling at me all evening after the wife came home from visiting family. Figured it out pretty quickly. Biggest resentment is the fact I saved that little fucker from a shelter only for him to grass me up at the first opportunity.

FAV: 12,425 RT: 217

To the young lady who stopped to chat as I stood rooted to the spot with my dog: I wasn't observing the birds in the tree, I was desperately trying not to shit myself. Thanks to your intervention, I ultimately failed.

FAV: 3,264 RT: 46

Talking to Dogs

There's a concept in computer science called 'rubber-ducking' where you explain your problem to a plastic toy on your desk and speaking it all out loud helps you find the solution. Dogs work just as well AND squeezing them too hard makes similar noises.

When I'm working from home, I like to have meetings with my dog about projects I'm leading. I pretend she's giving me encouragement and that she thinks I'm doing an amazing job. Weirdly it really helps and I've just gotten a work award for performance.

FAV: 10,345 RT: 274

I'm scared of confronting my wife so when I need to say something that may cause an argument I do it from another room in our dog's voice pretending that it's him so she'll be angry with him and not me. It doesn't work.

FAV: 4,226 RT: 83

HAVE YOUR SAY

~~~~~~

At least these replies aren't that photo of a dog going 'what a lovely day on the inter...' 'GOOD LORD!'

When he was a puppy, my brother's dog ate my glasses whilst I slept. I never understand how. I only know this because he shat them out and they were nearly completely intact. Do Specsavers want to use this as an ad for their value range?

@Specsavers: No

Every time I walk back from the shop I always kick a loose stone from my neighbour's drive along the street into my own drive. I'm stealing their gravel one stone at a time.

So you're winning on aggregate?

Bought a PS5 but it lives at my grandma's house. The Mrs has no idea. She thinks I go to care for my grandma every day, but I actually go and play the PS5 for hours. Grandma is healthy and sometimes plays too. She's promised to take it to her grave.

Why would she take it to her grave? She's not going to be able to get it connected to wi-fi when she's in there...

Only game played in there will be Worms

Thou Shalt Obtain Self Awareness and Laugh at Thine Own Uselessness

Self-knowledge
is easy to come by.
Just look at yourself
naked in front of a mirror and
shout 'loser'. Done that?
Right, you now know
you're easily led.

We are lucky enough to be able to afford a cleaner. However, part of me is really embarrassed that they'll think we're dirty so I always clean before they come. Must be the easiest money they make all week.

Police pulled up next to me a few days ago as I had stopped in what I now know is a red light area. I was playing Pokémon but when told by the officer to stop wanking and move on I apologised instead of showing him that I was playing Pokémon.

After I got blind drunk on a works night out, a workmate kindly put me up. I got up in the middle of the night, naked, to go for a piss, thinking I was at home. I turned left for the toilet as usual, fell down the stairs, shat myself and broke a toe.

I Feel So Much Cringe I Could Die

It's quite OK to stop dead in the middle of the supermarket and want to die over something dorky you said 20 years ago. Just do it quietly away from the meats.

Colleague announced she was going on maternity leave. I pointed to her belly and jokingly said, 'Well I didn't want to say anything.' She was adopting the baby.

**I was well into my 30s before
I realised that when
Neil Armstrong said 'It's one
small step for man, one giant
leap for mankind' he didn't
actually do a small step
followed by a giant leap.**

As a naive student I asked a dealer if I could pay for my weed with a cheque.

The first time I felt a girl's boobs when we were teenagers, I patted her on the back afterwards as a thank you. Mortified about it ever since.

At the the office party, followed my boss into the toilet thinking it was gender neutral because of the stupid arty stick figures on the door. It was the men's loo and he looked horrified and mumbled 'Err, hmmm, no, no thank you, thank you though.' I'm looking for a new job.

Went to a colleague's funeral the other day. We all lined up to hug and console his wife following the service. I said my words of solace but as the hug ended I felt the urge to say something else. 'Thank you for letting me come, I had a great time.' Have been cringing ever since.

My husband refers to a tube of anti-itch cream as 'bum-hole lotion' within the private confines of our home. I have just absent-mindedly asked for the same in a crowded Boots. I can never return.

When I was younger, I once told a bouncer that my dad owned the club, trying to blag my way in because I had no ID. Looked great in front of the massive queue and my friends. Got taken in to the 'VIP' area. Which was the rear exit. The bouncer turned out to be the owner.

FAV: 14,457 RT: 185

I Have an Avoidant Persoanlity

Who likes dealing with stuff? Psychopaths, that's who. The correct response to the world is to bury one's head in the sand and hope the bad thing passes.

Whenever I go to a bar or restaurant with my wife I always open the door for her and allow her to go in first. This looks like chivalry, but really I just don't want to have to speak to the person who greets you and asks if you have a reservation.

FAV: 10,358 RT: 159

I have a crush on the cleaner in my office, so much so that if I need to have a poo during the day, I'll drive the 34-mile round trip to go at home, just in case she goes in to clean the toilet straight after I've been in there. I'm a 60-year-old head of department.

FAV: 2,993 RT: 27

Back in the 90s I used to buy pirated porn VHS tapes from a shop in Soho. One time the bloke behind the counter gave me an extra free tape as he said to me, 'I always look after my best customers.' Mortified. Never returned.

FAV: 3,598 RT: 45

I've been going to a local bar for a few years. Recently, the owner introduced himself as he's seen me a lot. He was really nice and introduced me to the main group of regulars. We agreed that we would all be friends. Now, I avoid going in there and I go to a different bar.

Accidentally got off the bus two stops early last night because it was so dark and rainy I couldn't see. Realised it wasn't my stop the second the doors opened but I'd rung the bell and walked down the stairs and the bus was packed so I was too embarrassed not to get off.

I wasn't 100 per cent sure of my girlfriend's name for 7 months. Her name can either work on its own or be short for something else. We got together 2 weeks before COVID so I had to wait until lockdown ended to check her ID because I was too scared to ask.

I Just Like to Create Chaos

Sometimes it's fun to be the world's mildest troll.

Sat behind a guy in the pictures, he was 10 minutes away from winning an eBay auction. I found the item and began a bidding war until the last minute. The guy won but he won by paying about £25 more than I assume he anticipated paying, I was highly amused by my own doing.

I used to go to the pub and every now and then ignore an old woman I usually spoke to. The next time I saw her, I'd apologise for my ignorant twin brother's behaviour and she'd buy me a drink for being the 'nice one'. She went to her grave thinking I had a twin brother.

FAV: 3,912 RT: 62

Sometimes when I make a cup of tea at work, I casually bin the teaspoon. I've done this so often, that after months there are none to be found on our floor. I revel in the consternation caused and consider myself an agent of chaos. I manage a department of forty-seven people.

FAV: 4,870 RT: 78

If somebody's pissed me off at work, instead of my usual 'kind regards' I'll sign off my emails to them with 'regards'. Everybody knows a plain 'regards' really means 'fuck you', right?

FAV: 7,888 RT: 219

I Know I'm Lazy, Shut Up

It's smart to be lazy. The early bird gets eaten by the fox.

I once paid £3.99 to stream a film on Amazon because I couldn't be arsed to get up for the DVD I had on the shelf not 15ft away.

FAV: 50,613 RT: 1,256

I transferred my husband £5 the other day to pass me a bottle of wine from the kitchen counter because I couldn't be arsed to stand up.

FAV: 10,415 RT: 145

£4.99 has come out of my bank account every month from Apple Services since 2015 and I'm too lazy/stupid to know what it is. At this point I'd be disappointed to find out the truth, so I just ignore it.

FAV: 4,917 RT: 63

I did so little on the couch yesterday my smart watch said I was asleep 2pm to 5pm.

FAV: 7,959 RT: 84

I Went Along with It – I Guess This Is My Life Now

It just takes a small lie, or not correcting an assumption, and from that your entire life can grow.

My boyfriend told me he'd really like to try drag race. So for his birthday I got us VIP tickets to a drag show, we met the queens, he even got the chance to dress as a queen and go on stage with them. He went along with it all but later told me he actually preferred motorsport.

FAV: 21,780 RT: 482

My partner meets men online for sex to supplement her income while she studies law. Have to pretend I'm cool with it but I'm not. And terrified she will leave me once qualified. I spend my evenings arguing and raging with strangers online about a football team I don't even support.

I have the same name as an economist who is a expert in Japan's markets. I often get emails for him asking for quotes or predictions on the Yen. I reply with predictive text. One quote made the financial pages of a national paper.

Girlfriend caught me taking some pills and asked what they were. I was too embarrassed to admit they are hair loss treatment, so lied about having a heart condition. She told all her family how brave I am and how much she worries about me. It's been too long to own up now.

Some years ago my bank misprinted Dr instead of Mr on my statement. It was then changed to Doctor and is still on my card. I've taken out loans which I never would have been allowed as Mr.

Having accidentally called out an ex's name during sexy time, I managed to convince my fiancée it was a fantasy about my celebrity crush. Now 18 months into pretending I have a passion for Lorraine Kelly.

Eight years ago I found a rubber duck in my desk drawer and joked to colleagues that I collect them. They started buying them for me and now I've got hundreds. Even clients joined in, giving me corporate branded ducks as gifts. For my 40th they had a whip round and bought a rare collectible.

FAV: 13,714 RT: 219

I had to fake a call to Virgin Media in front of my wife – including pretending to be on hold for 10 mins – after porn appeared on the telly while the kids were watching. I'd accidentally screencast it while enjoying a private moment upstairs.

FAV: 11,808 RT: 207

When I was 17 I made the excuse for being off work that my sister had died in a car accident. A guy in my department became my best friend and every year he sends me a message telling me that he's thinking of me. I'm now 52.

FAV: 6,122 RT: 68

My wife bought me one of those wearable blankets with a hood you see advertised on Facebook. I had no interest in the item, but secretly fancy the fuck out of the woman that models it and she saw me watching the ad. Now I have to wear it in the evenings and I look a right idiot.

FAV: 5,798 RT: 75

I Am a Fat Bastard

If you want to lose weight, chop an arm off.

One of the reasons I moved abroad was so that my mum could only tell me how fat I am once a year at Christmas. We get along splendidly on the phone when she doesn't see me.

FAV: 3,511 RT: 42

There are four branches of Greggs within half a mile off my office. I have a bacon roll for breakfast every morning from a different Greggs so the staff don't know I'm a greedy bastard. They think I come in as a treat once or twice a week.

FAV: 6,769 RT: 80

In the queue at the doctor's an old man joined behind. 'How long?' he asked. 'Not very,' I replied, thinking he was asking how long I'd been waiting. He then asked if I knew what I was having. I didn't see the point in us both being embarrassed so I said a boy. I'm now on a diet.

FAV: 3,555 RT: 47

I Am Getting Old

It's OK to age, the alternative is worse: death.

I got a fantastic handjob off the Mrs the other night. It was only when she'd finished that I noticed I was wearing slippers. I felt like such an old man.

FAV: 4,318 RT: 53

I'm a single lady of a certain age, so was thrilled to hear a wolf whistle from a young, attractive neighbour while walking past his house. I gave him a little wave with a smile, thinking, 'Still got it.' Then I realised he was just calling his dog back inside.

Once got pulled over by the police while jogging because I 'looked distressed'. Told them I was running, copper replies, 'Running... from...?' Had to explain I was just unfit, not being pursued by an attacker. Bought a treadmill after that, much less police harassment.

I've finally got to an age where I wear my glasses to watch my wife masturbate. Am I the only one or do people just not discuss this?

I Am Literally a Shit

Maybe if you are a shit and you've realised it, it's time to expand your ambitions into upper management?

When I worked at a restaurant, I'd book 5–6 tables myself at 9pm so there was less work to do and I could go home earlier.

When my kids get given money for their birthdays/ Christmas, I take a cut for myself. I consider it their contribution to our living costs.

FAV: 3,343 RT: 43

My brother always wet the bed in his mid-teens. It got so bad that my mum had to have a meeting with the school to see if he should go on the French exchange she'd paid for him to go on. He never wet the bed, it was me pouring water on his mattress while he was asleep.

FAV: 8,202 RT: 151

I Am Duh... Stupid

We all have moments where our IQ drops into single digits. If you want to feel like this for free, huff glue.

In the mid-90s, as teens with a shared love of *Red Dwarf* and Manic Street Preachers, we formed a band called The Manic Rimmers. We didn't realise.

FAV: 4,474 RT: 153

For years I've been buying cappuccino pods for my coffee machine. Only today have I realised that the brown pods are coffee and the white pods are milk. I always wondered why they tasted different but it turns out I've been drinking warm milk and black coffee.

FAV: 5,425 RT: 87

I have precisely ZERO idea what people are doing when they inspect their egg boxes at the supermarket. But for 20-odd years I've dutifully opened the box, nodded appreciatively and then put my eggs in the trolley without the faintest idea what the hell I'm doing or why.

I ordered a dildo off Amazon and after it turned up, I thoughtlessly stuck the suction cup to my head. The bruise on my forehead was so bad that I barely left my flat for a week.

FAV: 5,032 RT: 85

Saw a Tweet from a guy who had a similar problem sorting out an online account that I faced recently. Spent ages preparing my reply with advice on how to deal with it, even deleting my original message and rewriting it, only to realise I was replying to my own Tweet.

FAV: 3,543 RT: 59

Local cafe set up a hole in the wall system during lockdown. I hated the wooden stirrers they had so looked online for a reusable metal one. Ended up drawing plans for one and was going to get a CNC shop to make up a batch. Two days it took me to realise I just needed a spoon.

FAV: 6,141 RT: 112

As a kid I once asked in a restaurant if duck was considered sea food. Everyone takes the piss out of me for it now but at 29 I still think it's a valid question. I'm completely over it, though. Maybe.

FAV: 7,567 RT: 120

Trying to prove to my wife that use-by dates are a guide and to just do the sniff test. Had a fish pie that was four days out of date but smelled fine. I've spent the day either passed out in my shed shivering or shitting my soul into a bucket. Might have to rethink this.

FAV:12,661 RT:301

I Enjoy Simple Things and That's OK

Honestly it's OK to enjoy ordinary things.

Over 30 years later, I still get the piss ripped out of me because I asked for a fizzy orange drink with a meal on a lads holiday abroad.

FAV: 7,625 RT: 87

I've recently got into a train-driving sim on my PC. When another train goes past I look to check my wife isn't watching at the door, then give the other driver a little wave.

FAV: 4,425 RT: 81

Work in sales and I get a 10 per cent performance bonus every January. Wife thinks it is half that. We get 5 per cent to do something nice together. I get 5 per cent for me. I wish I could say it is used for hookers and blow but I've spent it on a pottery course.

FAV: 8,016 RT: 71

I work 50–60 hours a week as a lorry driver. When I come home to relax, I love to play Scania Truck Driving Simulator.

FAV: 4,106 RT: 58

I was called into a meeting with HR over white powder residue found on my desk by the cleaners. I was deeply embarrassed but had to come clean that at 48 years old I still enjoy a sherbet Dip Dap.

FAV:12,640 RT:257

I Am a Born Loser

Face it. You're never going to amount to anything.

In order to reduce my 10 cups of tea habit I started drinking gravy. I now have a 15 cups of gravy a day habit.

FAV: 4,231 RT: 131

On a dating app, if I see a woman I like, my extremely low self-esteem tells me that she won't be interested in me. This stops me from swiping right. However, swiping left would lower my self-esteem even further. So, instead, I shut down the app.

FAV: 2,996 RT: 42

Friends are coming round tonight for a Chinese. They are bringing their daughter with them. She once told my daughter that our house stinks and is really messy. I am now on my hands and knees cleaning the kitchen floor to prove her wrong, a fucking 12-year-old. I'm so pathetic.

FAV: 13,794 RT: 141

I Do Drugs Because I'm Rock'n'Roll Like Shakin' Stevens

Everyone loves a drugs story, you know the ones, it was so funny, oh you had to be there. Hopefully a few of these are better.

As a naive 21-year-old, I was followed down a street in Amsterdam by a man repeatedly saying 'Charlie?' I answered, 'No, Jeremy' because that is my name.

FAV: 16,194 RT: 276

A man next to me left a baggy behind getting off the train. It looked like a big bag of weed so I put it in my pocket. I didn't want to look in public so I kept it in my pocket for about 30 minutes before I got home and smelled it. It was poo, most likely a dog's.

I once chucked up into a urinal when the two Es I had just taken hit a bit hard. They were £20 a pop back then so I did what seemed the right thing to do. I picked them out of the urinal, washed them briefly under the tap and took them again. Happy days.

On recent coke binge, was really horny and went onto a hook-up site. Got talking to a guy who wanted a guy to sleep with his wife while he watched. Went along and met up. Left 10 minutes later, was like trying to put a wet noodle through a keyhole. Shouldn't have had that extra gram.

When I put a teaspoon of honey in my tea, I always hold it at the surface for a few seconds to warm it up so it stirs in better. It feels like I'm doing heroin.

I live in South London and sometimes I fill little baggies with chalk and just leave them on benches or on top of bins. I like to imagine that some poor sod occasionally picks one up and tries to use the contents, thinking it's coke.

I Am Deffo Not an Alcoholic

Being a functional achoholic is better than being a unfunctional alcholic.

Whenever my wife and I share a bottle of wine, she always checks I pour equal measures. When she's satisfied I ask her to sit down while I bring over the glasses. I then gulp down a large mouthful from my glass and surreptitiously top it up. Done it for years.

FAV: 3,370 RT: 21

I got so drunk last night that I forgot I was vegetarian and went home with a large chicken kebab.

FAV: 5,145 RT: 86

I've had a pint in the pub while on my lunch break most days for about 10 years. I don't see it as like a 'dependency' thing or a bad thing. I just don't see the point in sitting at my desk having a meal deal when I could go the pub and watch Sky Sports News for an hour.

FAV: 11,573 RT: 138

I Stopped Drinking

The downside of stopping drinking is the dying of thirst.

My family and friends think I stopped drinking due to mental health. The truth is I worked as a bouncer and I see how fucking annoying people are when they are drunk and don't wish to put others through that.

FAV: 4,478 RT: 49

Quit drinking six months ago. The effects are amazing. I am thinner, handsomer, a better employee, a better parent, a better lover and generally more productive and happy. Gonna start up again, though, I miss my drinkies.

I Am Living With a Secret

If you've got a secret, trained Fesshole operators are waiting for your call.

When my daughter was born, my wife insisted we call her Jenna, which was one of the names I originally suggested. Twenty years on, neither of them know the name was inspired by my favourite porn star of the time, something I deeply regret to this day.

My mate often talks about what a great pal I was during his greatest heartbreak in 2008, including how I immediately removed his ex off my Facebook. Truth is it was her who removed me after I tried my luck with her less than 24 hours after they split.

I'm 5'9" but insecure about my height, so I've always worn 'lifts' in my shoes. With a pair of Nike Air Forces, I'm 6'. I met my girlfriend with these lifts in. Now I can't take my shoes off around her. I've kept my shoes on for almost two years now.

In the 90s my mum bought a *Full Monty* birthday cake. We opened it and added a marzipan cock and balls under the marzipan hat, complete with chocolate shavings as pubes, then re-sealed it. Mum went apeshit. She got a refund and apology from the supermarket.

When my wife and I gave notice to get married, we had to show a bank statement as proof of address. I was up all night photoshopping out the OnlyFans payments.

One Christmas morning, me and my boyfriend were having a spoon in bed under the duvet. My younger brother burst in saying happy Xmas and took a photo. We now have a lovely photo of us in which my boyfriend has just slipped his cock inside me.

I Have to Live With the Weight of This Terrible Guilt

If you want to not feel guilty the secret is to push all the bad feels into a corner of your mind and then play Windows Solitaire for months. Hey, don't knock it until you've tried it, there's some really great versions of Solitaire out there.

When I was 13 I stole a Cadbury's Creme Egg from a news agent. I felt so bad I went back the next day, paid for two of them and put one back when the server wasn't looking.

Aged 14, on a frosty night I wrote the name of my current crush on the roof of a random car. Turns out it was my mum's best friend's car and the name was that of her husband who had died six months previous. She was devastated. I still feel really bad about it.

In 2016 I saw my best mate's kid out playing on his bike. Drove up behind him to beep the horn and give him a fright, but accidentally hit him. Checked to make sure he wasn't badly hurt then drove off. Every year since I've spent more on his Christmas present than my own son's.

Secret Shame

These people's shame is only partially secret now – you know who you are.

Probably the lowest point of the early years after my divorce was me in the kitchen at 11pm, drinking whisky, some meatballs cooking in the deep fat fryer, having a wank straight into the kitchen bin.

At my mate's wedding someone said his sister was pregnant. Being a bit pissed I rubbed her belly and congratulated her. I forgot he had another sister. After deciding not to kill myself I approached his other sister and repeated the above. I also forgot he had a third sister.

Had a wank downstairs while my wife was asleep. Couldn't find the tissue so finished in my hand. Then heard her heading downstairs. Panicked so did the only thing I could think of and ate it. I'm sorry to every woman who I ever made do that.

FAV: 12,833 RT: 289

A car backed into me and I caught it all on my dashcam. My insurance company asked for the footage but I told them I'd accidentally deleted it. Really, I was too embarrassed to send it to them because you can hear me pretending I'm on the Graham Norton show in the background.

FAV: 7,288 RT: 116

A few years ago I was caught short in Waterstones and nipped into the disabled loo. A member of staff saw me leaving it and in a guilty panic I did an appalling impression of a disabled person all the way to the lift.

FAV: 3,196 RT: 47

I was walking home from town once and came across the most beautiful bouquet of flowers left by the side of the road. It seemed such a pity to leave them there, so I took them home. Where my daughter kindly pointed out that I'd taken them from the scene of a fatal accident.

FAV: 3,767 RT: 57

Had to go to A&E to get girlfriend's love egg removed from my arse. Gave my old housemate's name and DOB so it wouldn't show on my records. Still wonder if he ever found out. Sorry, Nigel.

FAV: 6,274 RT: 101

I have a butter knife I got from my German grandparents. Everything about is is perfect: balance, blade, handle size, spreadability. It just happens to have an eagle carrying a swastika on it. I have to hide it every time I have guests over.

The Real Reason I'm Doing it

People's stated motivation and actual motivation are often two different things.

I've volunteered to cook Christmas Day lunch for the homeless for the last seven years. As much as I care about homeless people, I do it because it's an excuse not to spend the day with my relatives.

My wife loves the fact I've started walking the dog more early each morning. Truth is they've installed a death slide/zipline in the park and I love going on it to start my day.

I've recently joined the gym under the pretence I am shifting some unwanted weight. Real motivation is I am 100 per cent certain my marriage will end this year and I need to be in shape for when I'm back in the game.

We've All Done It

Stuff we've all done. Well, this caption writer anyway. Oh god.

I had to use incognito mode at work when doing a presentation, automatically typed in pornhub dot com out of habit in front of 100+ people.

FAV: 6,024 RT: 111

If I realise I'm walking in the wrong direction, rather than just turn around, I stop, look at my watch, move my head from side to side like I'm weighing up whether I have enough time to go wherever it is I'm pretending to go, pull a face, nod my head decisively and turn around.

FAV: 15,639 RT: 329

My wife is worried I'm unwell because I was off my food. Truth is I drank a pint of custard straight out of the carton about half an hour before dinner was ready.

FAV: 16,783 RT: 372

When I was 9 I broke my bedroom window. To prevent my parents seeing, I put a poster over my window. Well I'm now 18 and the other day, the poster fell off my window, revealing no crack whatsoever. I asked my parents about it and they said they'd fixed it two days after it happened.

FAV:38,809 RT:643

HAVE YOUR SAY

~~~~~~

Here's some replies to fesses that we enjoyed more than
'Is that you dad'?'

Shat myself while out walking, pulled off my boxers and lightly buried them in a wood. A year or so later, a body was discovered in the same wood. Thinking my soiled kecks might be found as 'evidence', I went to the police station and explained. They're probably still laughing.

You're the number two suspect

At 19 I spent a lazy Tuesday stoned and railing three gorgeous friends. I'm 32 now and we all still live in the same town. They have all gone on to have very successful careers, families, everything, and I am a bricky left feeling like that Tuesday was the day my life peaked.

Keep hanging on in there mate, there's mortar come

I bought too much coke and couldn't finish it and
I was flying the next day, so I stored it in the airport toilets.
I came back a few weeks later and was still there!
Winning and sorted for Xmas.

Presume it had gone flat by the time you got back?

My mum and dad divorced and he started seeing someone
younger about two years later. He finally introduced her
only for me to realise I'd met her before. He popped the
question recently and now I'm going to have to watch him
marry a woman I shagged up the arse on a Tinder date.

Will you be the ring bearer?

Thou Shalt Perceive a Bigger World Than Thyself

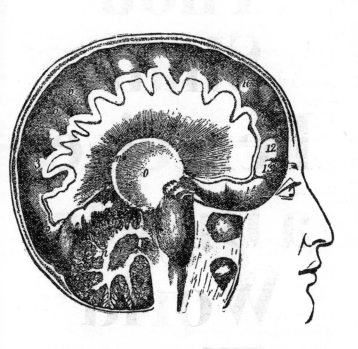

It's a big wide world out there
but you wouldn't want to paint it.

Missed getting on the tube that was blown up at King's Cross station in the 7/7 London Underground bombings by seconds, because I didn't run for it as I was tired from staying up late fixing a mate's laptop that was infected with viruses from him trying to find free porn.

I'm a musician with perfect pitch. For years I've been farting the note A#. I recently lost a load of weight and it's shifted up two semitones to C. This makes me so happy.

I'm a bald white guy, and since I went bald I always smile at ethnic minorities to show them I'm not a neo-nazi skinhead.

Celebrity Corner

If you'd like to be a celebrity the trick is to be good-looking and have rich parents. For the rest of us, there's text-based media.

Boris Johnson recently visited our pub while on holiday. Fetched a new glass from the cellar so I could spit in his pint without him noticing. Little victories.

When about 13 or 14, my friend and I found it hilarious to climb down these two ladders on a pier near where we lived, lean back with our bums sticking out, and watch each other poo into the sea. My friend is now a MP.

Went as a guest to an event full of famous people last week. I'll be honest, I did look peng. While waiting outside this young woman asked me if I was famous. Of course I said yes and posed for a selfie. She'll be wondering the rest of her life who the fuck I am.

FAV: 4,462 RT: 43

I used to sleep with a guy who looked exactly like Bob Mortimer. Only, he was gay and Italian. Still not convinced it wasn't him leading a double life or doing an elaborate bit. Great in bed.

FAV: 3,991 RT: 73

Britpop Corner

In a short section that's more 90s Select *magazine than* Fesshole, *let's catch up with some indie stars of post-baggy shoegazing.*

After a failed attempt at 90s indie rock stardom, I ended up as an IT consultant. I hardly play guitar now but still carry plectrums with me in case of an indie rock guitar emergency that will inevitably lead to my triumphant return to the scene.

FAV: 6,053 RT: 86

For my music GCSEs, I was asked to write a song. I couldn't, so I pretended an Ocean Colour Scene song was mine. I got a C.

FAV: 5,628 RT: 68

I played in a fairly successful indie band
in the 90s and we had one big hit;
I've never told anyone before but its
based on the theme to *Rentaghost*.

FAV: 6,573 RT: 440

Was in a load of middle-of-the-road indie bands in the mid 2000s always on the brink of 'making it'. A couple of years after knocking it on the head, I saw that one of my fellow musical losers had joined Snow Patrol and married Courteney Cox. Fifteen years later and I'm still fuming.

FAV: 4,976 RT: 39

Politics

Let's keep it light shall we – a bit of politics, but not too much politcs, just enough to totally date this section if you read it in a few years and these names are dust in the wind.

Liz Truss is the first prime pinister under whose tenure I didn't get a shag since I lost my virginity during the Blair years.

FAV: 3,301 RT: 79

> I called my boyfriend's balls his Squishy Sunaks. He won't talk to me anymore.
>
> FAV: 5,209 RT: 165

After years of this bloke trying to sleep with me, I made a deal that if he voted Labour I would do the deed. He sent proof so I did, he later confessed he rubbed it out and voted Tory. I should've known better, what a awful Tory thing to do. The shame.

FAV: 11,534 RT: 238

School Daze

----

*If your school days were the best days of your life then did your
early 20s wrong.*

**In Year 6, my friend and I got sent to the headteacher
for playing with Lego rather than doing our
schoolwork. We were told to take the Lego model
with us. Head assumed our teacher was proud of
the model we'd built and gave us some gold stars
instead of telling us off.**

FAV: 14,231 RT: 154

In junior school I submitted a poem about a mouse into
the class poetry competition. I got a 4/10, which must
mean Beatrix Potter was shit as I copied it straight out of
one of her books.

FAV: 9,596 RT: 154

**Around 16 years old on a pub night out, me and
some mates filled an upturned traffic cone with
fresh piss, leaned it up against a particularly cuntish
schoolteacher's front door, rang the doorbell and
ran away. Any guilt I feel today is outweighed by the
genius of the move.**

FAV: 5,039 RT: 83

Intrusive Thoughts

You can't control the thoughts that appear unbidden in your mind, and once you've read these, maybe you'll suffer from them too.

I like to pretend to be dead when my wife comes home. She tickles me and we both laugh. Now I'm terrified that one day I will actually die and she'll tickle my corpse.

FAV: 10,003 RT: 220

I left my favourite jacket at the World Trade Centre in August 2001. They said they'd mail it out to me but never did. I'm still bitter about it, it's all I can think about whenever I see 9/11 footage.

FAV: 4,031 RT: 88

I think my girlfriend really wants kids but I'm so scared it'll turn out to be a little cunt who can't have toast unless it's cut a certain way. I can't be doing with shit like that.

FAV: 7,686 RT: 158

I sometimes think the absolute worst thoughts possible and then watch the people round me carefully. Based on a lack of reactions so far, I'm pretty sure no one is reading my mind, but it can't do any harm to keep checking.

FAV: 3,970 RT: 82

When I was 14, I stayed at a friend's house whose dad owned a popular bakery. While making breakfast, he bossed me out the way and told me I was buttering the toast wrong. To this day, I don't know what I was doing wrong, but I recall this memory EVERY time I make toast. I'm 32.

When a woman sits next to me on the bus I always take it as a sign that I don't look like a rapist or a serial killer. Not looking like a rapist or a serial killer is definitely something I strive for, so it's nice to occasionally get validation like this.

Poetic Justice

Some stories have a complete beginning, middle and end and there's comeuppance for the moral wrong-doer.

Me and my wife decided to try an open relationship. I absolutely hate it and haven't slept with anyone. She's having the time of her life, though, and fucks other guys 2–3 times a week. I'd lose her if I told her to stop but I'm so sad.

I once told a naive school friend that the end of year party was Disney-themed fancy dress. It wasn't. The joke backfired when he turned up dressed as Cinderella, got swamped with attention from all the girls I fancied and became a legend in the school. I so wish it had been me.

Pulled on a boozy night out 20 years ago. I bought drinks all night and a greasy kebab – got my oats. Morning after, miles from home, skint and no bank card, lifted £10 from her purse, called a taxi and left. Guess who's joined my gym? Her daily stares almost paralyse me. Haunted.

I'm an introvert, but first day into a new job I met a gorgeous girl, so acted with loads of energy to charm her. Six months later, nothing happened and I'm exhausted every day trying to maintain the facade.

Played FIFA with my 12-year-old son. He beat me 12-1. Was fuming, so for last few weeks I've been secretly practising after he's gone to bed. Just had a rematch. Lost 14-0.

Thought I was funny stealing milk from someone's porch at 5am after a session. They posted a Ring doorbell video on Facebook. I had to go ask them to take it down and apologise.

During one night of passion with a young lady, she asked if I wanted to try anal. Eagerly I said yes. Imagine my surprise when a few moments later she jabbed her thumb up my bum hole with fast and extreme force.

I stole a first edition of *Harry Potter and the Philosopher's Stone* from my school library when I was 12. It's worth quite a bit now but I can't sell it as it has a 'Property of' stamp on the inside cover.

As a teen, I was doing gang signs in the mirror since I really wanted to be a cool thug. My mum walked in, so I lied I was practicing sign language. To help me learn, she signed me up for classes every Tuesday.

Digital Disconnect

The strange, sometimes parasocial relationships we have with people and technology.

I drink alone in the pub. Every time I return to my table I see my phone has lit up and I get a glimmer of hope it's a text from a friend. It's not, it's my bank telling me I've just spent money on the pint I bought.

Several years ago I followed someone on Twitter who I thought was my friend's mum. We've had several long exchanges about her daughter. Today she tweeted a photo of her daughter and it's not my friend. I have no idea what to do.

A mate shares his Netflix with various friends. Last year he changed his password to kick someone off for never calling him by changing his password from Badger21 to Badger22. Never call him anymore, just got booted without warning. Logged in fine with Badger23 though.

FAV: 3,981 RT: 27

I never remembered a guy's name I played sport with. Sometimes we'd exchange pleasantries and agree to visit the pub to watch sport. One day we met in the street and he said, 'You have my number, right?' He dialled mine and we both stared at my screen as 'Bloke calling' flashed up.

FAV: 4,414 RT: 54

I have a similar email address to an American guy, I get a lot of his mail. He seems like a bit of a dick – Republican, Harley Davidsons, strip clubs. I often respond and in 2013 I severely delayed his house purchase by demanding that his realtor sent me nudes.

FAV: 4,095 RT: 69

Language Differences

Britain is a country seperated by one language. Well, two. Well, three. Four, actually. Oh god, there's Cornish too. So that's five, we give up.

I'm Scottish and the Alexa device frequently mishears me. If it does it three times in a row, I unplug it as a punishment.

FAV: 4,403 RT: 101

I'm an atheist, but for a while had to attend a Christian church, where I was often complimented on how 'spirit-filled' I was when I 'spoke in tongues'. I was really reciting filthy jokes in Welsh.

FAV: 4,936 RT: 220

I moved to Portugal and learnt only the polite/formal way to speak. My cleaner and gardener tell me I am the only one that treats them so well and talks to them like equals, but in fact I just have no clue how to give them less polite instructions.

FAV: 11,026 RT: 143

An American girl really liked my Scottish accent and asked me to say 'Scottish things' to her while we had sex. I couldn't think what to say, so just started listing football teams. 'Raith Rovers. Partick Thistle. Hibernian...'

FAV: 23,976 RT: 737

I'm Welsh and my boyfriend's English. For Valentine's Day he surprised me by learning a Welsh-language love song and sang it to me. I haven't the heart to tell him that the song he chose is a deeply tragic song about a man begging a woman to tell him why she doesn't love him any more.

FAV: 7,178 RT: 107

Parents moved back to Ireland from the UK in the 70s, were all gung-ho for Irish language despite not speaking much. They messed around with Irish name spellings and chose something they thought sounded pretty when I was born. They accidentally called me the Irish word for cancer.

FAV: 5,115 RT: 95

Toilet Trouble

Let's talk about shit baby.

Due to anxiety issues and a small todger, I can't pee in a urinal. Instead I use a cubicle. However, I don't want other men to think I'm using the cubicle because of a small todger, or that I'm having a dump. So I take a couple of big sniffs to make it seem like I'm doing cocaine.

FAV: 6,434 RT: 123

My precious and perfect 6-year-old daughter only shits once a week and her turds are so big they don't flush. The only way I can get it to flush is to put my hand in the toilet and push it up the U-Bend as the toilet flushes. They don't tell you this stuff in any parenting books.

FAV: 10,268 RT: 127

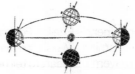

My proudest achievement is having four shits in four different countries in the same day. My marriage and the birth of my two daughters don't come close.

FAV: 5,715 RT: 111

I once went for a walk with a hangover in a local wood and felt the urgent need to empty my bum. I squatted over a shrub and dropped runny brown. A white rabbit then ran out, covered in my shit. It was 20 years ago but I still laugh to this day.

FAV: 3,482 RT: 54

Desperate and unable to find suitable facilities,
I once took a shit in a box in the back of my van.
For some unknown reason I then taped it shut,
wrote 'Do not open' on it and left it at the side
of the road. I still feel a weird sense of shame
and amusement many years later.

FAV: 10,700 RT: 82

Quite drunk, I went back to a girl's place. Needed to shit, went to deal with it. Went back to bed. Woke up before her and discovered I hadn't lifted the seat. A huge log was sat on there. I left.

FAV: 5,963 RT: 92

Started my last lockdown loo roll today. Turns out I stockpiled 26 months' worth.

FAV: 9,615 RT: 178

Sometimes when I go for a piss, I like to hold on the the end of my knob and start. When my cock inflates like a balloon I let go and try not to get covered in piss. No idea why, but it's a good game.

FAV: 3,631 RT: 40

I sometimes send a photo of my unflushed shit to my house WhatsApp chat, feigning anger and accusing one of my housemates of leaving it in the bathroom. It always causes arguments and I love it.

FAV: 1,455 RT: 19

My boyfriend never wipes his arsehole after having a shit and instead just washes himself in the shower at the end of the day. Can't call him out on it any more after five years. I'm packing my bags to leave tonight for this reason alone.

FAV:10,369 RT:164

So Why Do People Confess on Fesshole?

After a Fesshole Live show in London in 2022, a man came up to me, gripped my hand and asked why people contribute to this account. I said, 'Because it's funny.' He looked disappointed and said he had hoped that I would have a better answer than that. So we asked contributors to Fesshole why they confessed. Seventy-eight people replied and we're printing a few highlights here. Maybe one of these answers will make more sense to the man from the show.

'For the glory of having my filthy life out there and people not knowing that it's me.'

'To see how the world reacts.'

'People love to tell stories. Fesshole gives them the opportunity to share their comedy, vitriol, genius, stupidity and imagination with thousands of readers.'

'For the satisfaction of having my fess deemed worthy of publishing.'

'I confess because my boyfriend follows all my social media and questions everything. Confessing anonymously helps me vent without being judged.'

'Confess? This is my therapy, man.'

'To outdo other confessions within the Fesshole universe.'

'I shared something with a Twitter account that I could not tell my therapist. The comments were full of compassion. I needed it. Thank you.'

'Anonymity in a social media age is an interesting concept. What if I wanted to tell people something but them not know it was me? My early fess about gaming Sainsbury's online shopping (or more accurately, "supermarket fraud") allowed me to do this.'

'Search for community maybe? Someone could read about my weirdness and say "Hey, I'm weird like that, too."'

'Sometimes I just want to make up the most awful thing I can think of and, deservedly, get called horrendous names for it.'

'I confess because it's stuff I can't tell my family or friends. You've never bloody published it, though, so it can't be that shocking.'

If you wish to further explore why people want to confess, Fesshole looks forward to reading your PhD dissertation.

Write the reason why you confess on Fesshole in here using a biro, or draw a picture of a sausage dog, whatever.

Thou
Shalt
Eventually
Die

*Death comes to us all,
but the important
bit is to keep laughing,
like these people.*

Secretly looking forward to the older generations passing on so we can stop pissing about with Christmas cards.

Since turning 40, I've bought the hardback copy of my favourite author's new books instead of waiting for the cheaper paperback in case I die before it's released.

Every December I gave my dad £150 or so. It was to buy Xmas gifts for my wife. Not from him, but from me. He had such an incredible talent for gift buying. I'm awful at it. I was always so grateful. He died in June. I have no idea what to get my wife for Xmas this year.

Ashes to Ashes – The Funny in Funerals

Everybody loves a good funeral. When we go, we'd like to be left on top of a hill and picked apart by crows. The circle of life and all that.

After scattering Mum's ashes, our family all went for dinner together. While washing my hands, I felt an object under my fingernail and sucked it out. Only when I rejoined the others did I realise I'd just eaten my mum.

I'm not spiritual or religious at all,
I never have been. But since my nan
died I've been scared to have a wank
just in case she's watching over me.

A uni mate recently passed away and a group of us took his ashes on a pub crawl. We snorted some of his ashes. It's what he would have wanted.

> **Mum died in September. She never left England, hated travelling anywhere, hated extremes of heat/cold, hated 'foreign' food. I travel a lot and take some ashes everywhere and leave them in places she would've fucking hated. It's a big world out there and she's finally seeing it.**
>

Dealing With That Moment of Death

Saying goodbye to a loved one is hard, so why not instead block all their calls in their last few months of life?

My mum just texted telling us that our grandfather just died. She used the crying laugh emoji. I'll wait a few days before taking the piss

My mum just called me to tell me my uncle died today. I am in absolute shock as I thought he died years ago, and now I'm worried I won't ever be able to ask who the person was that actually died years ago.

My mum died unexpectedly last month and it's devastating. However, I find comfort in knowing that the *Daily Mail* have now lost one more customer.

FAV: 6,301 RT: 104

Dementia Is a Wicked Curse

----

*There's nothing funny to say about dementia -
it's the cruelest end.*

My wife is 68 and riddled with dementia. She doesn't know who our kids are anymore, she doesn't know who her sisters are, she barely knows who I am. But of course, OF COURSE, she still remembers that affair I had in 1994. And no, she still won't let it go.

FAV: 90,642 RT: 4,243

My mother's confession – she's 91 with advanced dementia and does this thing where she suddenly slumps, goes limp and unresponsive. First time, she was with my sister who thought she'd passed. She's just done it now. Turns out she's playing dead and thinks she's being funny.

FAV: 20,197 RT: 370

Mum has dementia, and gets really anxious that she hasn't bought me enough Christmas presents so every year I wrap up a bunch of stuff I already own and tell her she bought it for me. This year Mum 'bought' me fantasy novels, a jacket, kitchen stuff and a copy of *Pokémon Sword*.

FAV: 26,567 RT: 313

Dead Pets

Mourning for animals is like mourning for humans but it's quicker and you rarely miss humans for balls they no longer fetch.

I'm a grown man but when my dog died I still went on my evening dog walk. I said it was for exercise but I'd bawl my eyes out doing the same walk as normal with her lead, she just wasn't attached to it anymore.

FAV: 26,996 RT: 333

My dog died recently and every night I now put a blanket over the bottom part of my duvet, so it still feels like they're there when I go to sleep

FAV: 9,979 RT: 68

My wife's beloved cat passed away three months ago and I buried it outside. This morning our new spaniel puppy was covered in mud, eating something in the garden and refusing to come in. I've had to tell the wife it was a turkey carcass and do a quick reburial.

FAV: 3,871 RT: 36

Online Executor

Remember: if a loved one dies, quietly tidy up their search histories. It's your solemn final duty.

I'm a straight guy with terminal cancer. I've not got long left. From my hospital bed I recently told my best mate to think of me every time he gets sucked off, knowing full well that's going to ruin every blowy he receives from now until he's dead also.

FAV: 21k RT: 423

**When clearing out my dad's house
after he died, I kept his wheelchair.
We take it to Alton Towers and
don't have to queue for anything.
Thanks, Dad.**

FAV: 9,710 RT: 156

Father-in-law passed away and I found so much porn while clearing out his room. Glad I got to it before his widow or my wife did, as not only do I have loads of vintage smut, I also didn't want that to be one of their last memories of him. I got your back, Pete.

While clearing out my late uncle's place, I found his porn collection. He also had a notebook full of hookers' numbers and 500 quid in crisp 20 quid notes in it, with a Post-It telling me to enjoy myself. I bought a Lego MindStorms set with the cash.

My dad and me had pet names for each other. He was Dickhead, mine was Dickhead Junior. He died, very unexpectedly. The fact that the last thing I ever said to him was 'See you soon, Dickhead' always makes me smile and horrifies anyone I tell that story to.

Fifteen years ago mate died of cancer. He arranged with me and three other lads to go in suits to his funeral, speak Italian and say, 'We're gonna miss you, Boss,' to pretend he was secretly a gangster or something. His mother called the police.

I'm the only person in my family that knows my dad died in a gay brothel in Spain.

I was madly, insanely jealous when my husband's ex got in touch and asked him over to her place. He said she sounded really upset so he went. Turns out she was terminally ill and died a couple of months later. I am so ashamed.

It is not that I fear death, I fear dying in a newsworthy way, because all my best pics are on dating apps. Every woman in a 100km radius is going to be like, 'Hey, that's the bloke who was begging for pegging.'

My wife occasionally asks me, 'What would you do if I died?' I don't have the heart to tell her that I've got a list in the Notes app on my phone.

The fiancée and I are looking to buy a house together. Our favourite game right now is to decide whether someone has died in a house based on the pictures on Rightmove. Major tells are a grab rail in the shower and a stairlift. We regret nothing.

SO WHAT HELL IS 'FESSHOLE LIVE' THEN?

One of the most unexpectedly delightful outcomes of opening a jokey confessions account has been the opportunity to do live shows, all encouraged by producer Giles Gear. Giles messaged me saying he'd recently been putting on shows with such greats as shouting expert Brian Blessed and parish councillor Jackie 'You have no authority here' Weaver, and would I like to have a go?

We booked the first show in London's Soho for April 2022 – the idea of people attending a confessions night and then spilling into the filthy streets to buy drugs and illicit massages amused us, and we were ecstatic to sell 200 tickets.

Friends said, 'Fesshole is a Twitter account, how can that be a live show?' Well, we figured some of it shouldn't be too hard. Get up like Dave Gorman and present some slides showing the funniest confessions – we've done plenty of work presentations, what's the difference, really?

But the thought clanged: if you're going to do a live show about confessions you need audience confessions! It HAS to be about the room.

So I set up a Google form and asked ticketholders to submit their fesses and boy did people like doing that. I got 54 entries, more than one quarter of the audience wanted to confess. The night itself went past in a blur. I remember a woman getting on stage and telling us how an operation had ruined her love of anal sex. Did that really happen?

So here's some stuff we've learned by taking the show around the country...

IN MANCHESTER we met a lady who accidentally turned her son Tory.

IN BELFAST we met a man who has a vigilante attitude to dogshit and walks around with small white flags to stick in it, to put up shaming photos on Facebook.

IN LONDON we met a man who had accidentally killed a swan by throwing a turf of grass at it. Another gent in the room had intentionally killed a tree that was impinging on his sunbathing light. (People were much more down on the premeditated killing of the tree, rather than just the horrible outcome of a bit of tomfoolery.)

IN EDINBURGH we met a couple who very much wanted to tell us about how they didn't wash very often. And they were very into pegging.

IN BRISTOL we got the guy who invented the Badger Badger Badger Mushroom song, an early internet viral that B3ta fans will remember, on stage and singing.

IN NEWCASTLE with sweat pouring down the walls, we had a lady who told us, 'I once had an awful one night stand with a man that couldn't finish unless he had his nipples aggressively yanked on. Wanting it to be over asap, I obliged. Longest 20 minutes of my life.'

AND IN LEICESTER we had a lady tell us about her dad who had shit tattoos. So what? When we pressed a bit more, we realised that her dad was covered in Nazi tattoos and it was time to end this quite alarming conversation.

I really do implore you to come to the next show – every single one of them is unique because of the audience. It creates quite an extraordinary atmosphere in the room, having the very people confessing this stuff, confessing it live. So see you there, my Fesshole friends. And remember, it's all fun and games until someone actually confesses to a murder and I have to dob you in to The Filth.

LATEST FESSHOLE LIVE TICKETS ARE AVAILABLE BY CHECKING THE PINNED TWEET ON THE ACCOUNT

But
Thou
Shalt
Have
a
Happy
Ending

Let's finish this book with some fun

and heart-warming stuff because

who wants a downer ending?

How about a few stories of people

telling mild lies to make their

day more interesting.

I'm an accountant for HMRC, but when people ask me what I do I tell them I'm an accountant for MI5, I have no idea if MI5 have accountants as I don't do any of their taxes.

I visited the kebab house with a friend one night who's a copper they give a huge discount to. They assumed I was a copper too and now when I go in I also get a discount. Problem is they ask things like 'You not on duty tonight?' and I have to act all copperish.

Whenever I stay at a hotel I ask if there have been any messages left for me every time I pass by the reception. There never are any messages, but it makes me feel like James Bond. I doubt Bond would be staying in a cheap Travelodge though.

Not All Heroes Wear Capes

People being nice. It's nice to be nice, isn't it? Let's all do that random acts of kindness thing like it's the early 90s again. And bring back £15 Es that really get you mashed.

I'm a police officer. Saw a woman shoplifting food today. Watched her steal bread, milk and eggs, chocolate and other stuff. I accidentally forgot to do anything about it. Soz.

I work for Tesco. Our food bank donation bin is in a blind spot and I frequently put stuff in it from the shelves during my shifts without paying.

FAV: 75,361 RT: 1,552

Working for Council Tax, I received calls from people snitching on neighbours about working or partner in house. I listened intently and did nothing, passed nothing on and wrote nothing down. Can't be doing with grasses.

FAV: 20,855 RT: 757

I used to work in a well-known coffee shop. We had a really sweet regular who came in. He was blind. I didn't have the heart to awkwardly guide him through the card machine at the time, so I just did a high-pitched beep noise and let him go and get his drink for free.

FAV: 10,938 RT: 124

At a house party years ago I witnessed some lad rubbing his ball bags on numerous kitchen utensils, mainly from the cutlery drawer. It seemed pretty funny at first, but later that night, when the coast was clear, I did the right thing and put all the stuff in the dishwasher.

FAV: 3,827 RT: 31

In Year 10 I had to scribe a Maths GCSE for someone who'd broken his arm. I was told to write down only what he told me, but he was shit at it so I wrote some better answers for him. I found out he got a C. I may have changed his whole life, but you're the only way I can confess.

FAV: 8,853 RT: 73

Friendship

In the words of the Spice Girls, 'friendship never ends' but they also suggested that you should 'get with their friends', which was rather too saucy for us, so what do they know?

The WhatsApp groups I am in with my best friends have got me through the last three years. During this time we have been consistently offensive to each other. I will never tell them how much I love them.

FAV: 7,085 RT: 162

Bit tame, but started a new job recently, me and the other alcoholic instantly clocked each other and we have a silent pact. If one of us is hungover the other one gives them the easy jobs out back where it's nice and quiet, and vice versa. It's the best friendship I've ever had.

FAV: 8,897 RT: 97

My wife caught me watching porn on my phone as I left sound on by mistake. I immediately reacted with 'My best mate sent me a link to stitch me up.' She texted him, laying into him that he was immature, as her parents were in the kitchen. He took the hit and said sorry. Cheers, Jay.

FAV: 16,856 RT: 147

Had builders in for six months. Job recently completed. I'm sad they're gone. Will miss the morning chat and having people in the house. Was half tempted to see if they wanted to catch up sometime and watch the World Cup, but that's weird and fucking creepy of me, so haven't.

FAV: 9,192 RT: 76

Took my 11-year-old daughter to a
football match. At the end she held
my hand walking through the crowds
and I couldn't remember the last
time this happened. My heart melted.
We have season tickets now. We never
leave early to beat the crowds.

FAV: 20,312 RT:213

Childish Lol

The joy of purile humour – never stop enjoying this stuff, it keeps you young.

When flying I get a cheap thrill from sitting in what I have deemed to be the 'boob seats'. Today is a particularly good day, I'm in 32F.

FAV: 5,452 RT: 81

I go to church every Sunday like a good Christian. When the congregation says 'Amen', I say 'gay men'. It's childish and I might also go to hell for it.

FAV: 3,961 RT: 67

Going out with a fairly religious girl, after a few months she broke up with me because I kept saying 'He has risen' every time I had an erection.

FAV: 9,717 RT: 239

When we set up our joint current account, I set the name in the app to 'Currant Account' so that when my husband asked why, I could say 'Oh, no raisin.' It's been three months and he hasn't noticed, and it's starting to grate every time I read it.

FAV: 4,543 RT: 86

Got invited to a Christmas carol concert at St Paul's Cathedral. Lovely evening and I still sing 'O come all ye faithful' with a slightly louder 'come' like I did at secondary school. I'm a 54-year-old CEO.

FAV: 3,536 RT: 33

Whenever I go into a shop selling Bluetooth speakers with my son, I hook my phone up to one and turn the volume right up. We then hide and use a fart app and let him play fart sounds through the shop. We both find it hilarious.

FAV: 6,176 RT: 124

Childhood Misunderstandings

We used to believe that cats were girls and dogs were boys. Admittedly we were 38 and a fully qualified vet.

Until the age of 28, I thought 'hump day' referred to sex. And that my dad didn't enjoy having sex with my mum most Wednesdays, as he'd tell me Thursday morning, 'Well, at least we've got hump day out of the way.' Never understood why he was sharing and dragging me into it.

FAV: 9,338 RT: 148

An irresponsible grown-up told me that spaghetti alphabet was all lower case when cold and turned into capital letters when heated up. Didn't realise it was bullshit until my twenties.

FAV: 4,844 RT: 152

When 6 years old, saw Beefeaters at the Tower of London. They had ER emblazoned on the uniform. Asked Mum what it meant, she said, 'It means the Queen'. Reasoned to myself that if that's what ER meant then a king would be IM.

FAV: 5,997 RT: 165

As a child I thought that 'jackpot' was short for jacket potato. Asking my dad why anyone would bother entering a quiz with a jacket potato as the top prize was one of the most embarrassing moments of my childhood.

In the pub with my dad and his mates when I was younger, one shouted 'he couldn't score in a brothel', everyone laughed so I joined in. My dad quizzed me as to what a brothel was. I explained in front of everyone 'It's where they make soup.' Still haunts me to this day.

All my life I thought when you did a 'moonie' you were supposed to spread the hole. Probably traumatised loads of people. Had to have it explained to me on my mate's stag do.

When I was six I went dinosaur hunting in the back garden. I found a set of bones and rebuilt them on the lawn. When I was done I showed my grandma. She told me they sent it to a museum in London. It was the family dog from before I was born and my grandad reburied it.

I was in my 30s when I found out that Rudyard Kipling did not make cakes.

One day when very young, I wanted to think about naked women, but I was afraid that a thought bubble like you see in cartoons would appear above my head. So all afternoon I banned everyone from coming into the front room while I laid on the couch thinking about tits.

FAV: 4,502 RT: 103

Whimsy

Just some whimsy to finish up as this book flies into the sun, driven by Danny and whatsherface from Grease.

Driving on the M1 yesterday I undertook a car from the Netherlands just so I could say that I 'passed the Dutchie on the left hand side'.

FAV: 11,106 RT: 408

Girlfriend questioned why I put my deodorant on like a big X on my body and I couldn't admit that it's because that's how Nick Frost does it in *Hot Fuzz*.

FAV: 13,869 RT: 441

Read in a Jack Reacher book that you shouldn't turn on the light that comes on in your car when you open the door as it's a sniper's dream. Not had it on for years and never been sniped. Winner.

FAV: 13,908 RT: 382

When I change the sheets I sing 'It's a nice day for some clean bedding' in the style of Billy Idol.

FAV: 4,956 RT: 161

I have a secret code word that only I know, in case I meet my time-travelling future self and have to confirm my future self's identity. I've kept it secret for 20 years.

I'm a 38-year-old man and when I arrange the soft toys on my daughters bed while making it, I'll position them in a way that they would be able to interact in case there is any consciousness in there.

Whenever my laptop battery says '48% remaining' I have a wry little smile to myself.

If I'm dishing up say, peas, and one stubborn pea remains in the pan, I'll go to great lengths to scrape around to make sure that pea gets served, not for economic reasons but because I worry about him getting lonely.

Whenever I'm eating sprouts, I silently pretend I'm a giant eating tiny cabbages I've just stolen from the villagers' fields.

Actually Sweet

Nice wholesome stuff to show that Fesshole isn't just here for the stories about shit and wanking. We have range. Bruce Hornsby & The Range.

Too much bad stuff on here, so my confession is that I love my partner. The best thing for me is that they are the first person I see in the morning and the last person I see before I fall asleep.

FAV: 13,796 RT: 272

Whenever I see Post-It notes on someone's desk at work, I carefully open them to the middle and write a nice comment like 'You're amazing' or 'I hope you're having a lovely day' so they find it down the line, like a pleasant surprise.

FAV: 5,365 RT: 120

At my local church there's a grave for a girl that died on Christmas Day in 1902 and I anonymously put flowers on her grave every Christmas.

FAV: 16.5k RT: 129

My mentor at work and I are both autistic. We're meant to spend a couple hours a month talking about how to improve my work. Usually she talks about her crochet projects and I talk about football while we have a cup of tea. It's my favourite part of the job.

FAV: 7,324 RT: 101

When I was a small child and went
shopping in supermarkets with
my father we often used to skip
down the aisles holding hands.
Now, on the rare occasion we
see each other and go shopping
we still do it. Me 53, he 71.

FAV: 17.3k RT: 308

An old guy at my golf club had cancer and used to joke that he wanted a hole in one before he dies. Par 3 on our course is a blind shot, I waited and ran onto the green, put his ball into the hole and ran off. He's passed now but that night was the happiest I've ever seen him.

FAV: 157,130 RT: 3,838

My wife doesn't know but I drop the answer to Wordle into casual conversation each morning. I like to think this subliminally helps her in the very competitive daily Wordle competition she has with her work colleagues. She's now winning.

FAV: 153,255 RT: 4,470

Lost a drunken bet and had to join a trainspotting group. They're honestly a lovely bunch of people and I've stuck with them. I couldn't care less about trains, but we do a nice walk and talk. Then I have to ooh and aah at a train and it's back to having a laugh.

FAV:12,011 RT:167

Once saw a very drunk young lad fall over and gave him a lift home. Turns out his mum had recently died. We played music from his phone and my car Bluetooth still lists him. It's still saved and I think good wishes whenever I see it, though he won't remember me. Merry Xmas, Ben x

FAV:27,990 RT: 328

There are very few good father role models in society. However, Bluey's dad has turned my life around. I am genuinely a better father and husband now I pause and think, what would Bluey's dad do?

My mum and dad died very suddenly. They were super kind people. Every couple of months I go into a cafe, buy all the cakes, tell them to give them to kids and say it's from them. I miss them so much but this way their names are said all day and people are made happy.

My twins, age 6, wake before me in the morning and go to to the toilet in my en suite. I pretend I am asleep as they always put their favorite teddy under my arm and kiss me on the head. I am a 47-year-old man and this is the best moment of my day.

The local lollipop lady is lovely and insists on helping everyone cross her road, regardless of age. I've actually started walking to work later to make sure I bump into her to ensure a positive start to the day. I'm a 41-year -old bloke.

My nephew fell over in front of me and my family. I picked him up and said, 'Why do we fall down? So we can learn to pick ourselves back up.' Whole family now think I'm the greatest uncle ever when in fact it was just a quote from *Batman*.

If you're reading this book at someone else's house (on the toilet maybe?) why not add your own anonymous confessions on this page?

Ten Things We've Learned Running Fesshole

Since Fesshole was launched in September 2019, two hundred thousand confessions have been submitted and I've read every single of one those eight million words. It's brought me terrible knowledge that no man should have.

1. There are a lot of men who have dark sexual desires for women Tory politicians

A few years ago you wanted to be dominated by Priti Patel: 'I'm a die-hard socialist but my biggest celebrity crush is Priti Patel. It's that goddamn smirk, just sends me under.'

Then it was Braverman: 'Had an incredibly erotic dream about Suella Braverman standing over me in a skintight PVC catsuit, yelling that I didn't belong here while whipping me.'

And more recently it's been Penny Mordaunt. 'I am conflicted, I fucking hate the Tories but I think that Penny Mordaunt is really hot. Having seen her sword-wielding at the Coronation, it was only the fact that I was in company that stopped me from knocking one out.'

It's presumably a masochistic fantasy and you all want to be told off by Matron and sent to bed with no tuck.

2. People can't tie their shoelaces

A remarkably common confession is people struggling with their shoes. 'I'm an adult and I still tie my shoelaces in the bunny loop method.' Many can't tie them at all: 'I'm 39 and still don't tie my shoelaces, I just tuck them into my shoes, ain't nobody got time for that.' I suspect the next big TV hit will be called 'How to Adult' and it'll teach basic skills to adults who've missed out because their own parents were too busy playing Candy Crush to parent properly.

3. Women are endlessly shoving toothbrushes in loos

The confession bin is overflowing with toothbrush abuse. 'My dickhead husband shouted me down in front of others. I proved him wrong. He didn't apologise. I cleaned the loo with his toothbrush.'

There are so many similar ones. 'My husband was cheating on me, his behaviour towards me was vile. So I used his electric toothbrush to clean under the rim of the toilet.'

Men probably need to start locking up their toothbrushes. Or stop being arseholes who cause women to exact petty revenge. Either one.

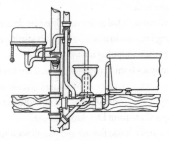

4. Men piss in sinks all the time

Possibly the most phoned-in confession is men's endless desire to tell this publication that they urinate into the washbasin. 'I piss in the kitchen sink about 76 per cent of the time,' says one gent. And then there's the positively threatening 'If I've been in your house and used the toilet I've pissed in your sink.' The truly alarming thing is by publicising it, we're influencing it, and turning into pissfluencers. 'I read a confession on here and, for some reason, decided to try it. I instantly felt bad. I don't think I can stop now, though. Pissing in the sink on trains really is much more convenient.'

Maybe swill out the sink a little, guys?

5. People like shouting 'Didn't happen!' a lot

Just because something is unusual doesn't mean it didn't happen, and anyway, we're not going to publish the mundane stuff, are we? Who would read that? We'll leave it to this submitter to say it best: 'Five of my posts have been on here now, every one is true but called false in the comments. The people who say it didn't happen have lived a very sheltered, boring life if they think these things could never happen.'

6. You should never use a hotel kettle

We're not quite sure if it's one guy who keeps submitting the same stuff or if the nation is filled with kettle pissers, but we see a lot of this: 'Sometimes when I stay in hotels I urinate in the kettle and empty it but do not rinse, so if you ever wonder why your coffee taste likes piss, it probably is.' As one submitter says, 'Sat in a hotel room, staring at the kettle. A mixture of disgust and wonder. I'm worried Fesshole has ruined me.'

7. There are a lot of men who probably should buy their own underwear

Confessions like 'When my wife is out I like to try on her underwear, I love it' are very common. We've spoken to a woman and she tells us, 'If that's your kink, buy your own and stop stretching mine, fatty.'

8. Men would get a lot more sex if they tidied up without being asked

This is certainly a common complaint from women –does it work? Who knows, but worth a go, chaps.

9. Grindr is mostly straight men just doing straight stuff with other straight men

'I secretly go and meet men I've met on Grindr when I tell my wife I'm off to football.'

'Married to my wife for 30 years. Two great kids. The epitome of marital bliss. But when I'm away at conferences I'm a complete Grindr slut.'

'Sometimes I meet guys on Grindr for a fuck. I don't find guys attractive but they are up for no-strings fun more than women. I class myself as straight.'

Obviously this is 2023 and absolutely fine and you should all live your best life.

10. The public are as funny as fuck

This, above everything, is the lesson of Fesshole. Turn to any page in this book, go to any tweet on the account. There's the public being hilarious.

And finally, here's to our reader who said this: 'I bought the Fesshole book optimistically thinking that the excellent and, crucially, true fesses I submitted that didn't get tweeted might have made the print version. No...'

We've just made your dream come true.

INDEX
~~~~~~
All the commandments and sub-commandments in order

Didn't happen...

What a terrible
day to have eyes...

Pics or it didn't happen!

Unfollowed!

Fesshole FAQ

Everybody asks the same questions.

Why didn't you publish my confession?

Many reasons, but a very common one is that it's very similar to one already published. There's only so many times we can shout about pissing in sinks. OK, one more time: 'I've been pissing in sinks for years, just the right height, although it can be cold on the balls. It saves loads of water and nice doing something you know you shouldn't be doing.'

Can I confess by directly messaging the account?

No, because that reveals your name, the only way to be anonymous is to use the form: https://bit.ly/add_confession

What's the stuff that you don't publish?

People tend to believe we're keeping the really exciting and
filthy stuff back, but really, we're giving you the best stuff. You'd
be very bored of this project if we published everything as there's a
lot of repetition and also men endlessly talking about wanking.
And we publish a lot of stuff about wanking already. Sorry.

You're just collecting all this stuff
to blackmail people, aren't you?

The anonymity is real. All we know about you is what you type.
Anyway, blackmail is messy, if you want to do fraud on the
internet it's simpler to buy a list of credit card numbers.

Will you move Fesshole to Blue Sky,
Mastodon, Threads or whatever
social network Elon Musk isn't running?

We'll probably expand it to other networks at some point
but you must understand we're incredibly lazy.

How can I just read three fesses per week
and for them to be the very best ones?

OK, no one is asking this but the answer is to subscribe to
the B3ta newsletter which we've written for the last 20+ years
and it features the best of Fesshole and the finest internet projects
made by our friends every week. https://b3ta.com/subscribe

THANKS TWO...

Briony Gowlett for putting up with the book being late. Sorry.

Antony Topping for agenting.

Giles Gear of Giddy Aunts for doing the Fesshole shows with me.

Chris Barker for doing design and keeping me entertained on DMs.

Hebtroco, that is, the two handsome men
Brant Richards and Ed Oxley for sponsorship of the tweets.

The b3ta collective of Wil Hadden, Matt Round, Monkeon
& HappyToast for helping keep the old website going
and finding new fun talent and jokes.

Kat for being the best human in the world.

Angus, Stanley and Max for being the three
other best humans in the world.

My parents Margot and David for having the foresight to
have a third child and very much the pair of them for giving me
space in my childhood to explore hobbies. What a gift.

Paul Lathe, Victoria Luck and Mushy Bees
because you all should be here for more bullshit.

Joseph Lenham because I know he'd have loved Fesshole
– sorry you missed it, old friend.

The Beatles for showing us the ideal on
how to live a creative life.

Bill Drummond for making acid house
and burning a million quid.

Everyone who contributed a confession – you know
who you are, and I don't because it's totally anonymous.
So I literally can't thank you by name. Sorry.

Leonard and Majel for the walks in the woods.
Bungle and Boop for catching the mice.

And remember:
FOLLOW @FESSHOLE NOW (and @anon_opin)

FIN
(DUS CRISPY PANCAKES)

❧ About the author ❧

Robert Manuel has made internet projects
for over twenty years, including B3ta.com
and various Twitter bots including
@anon_opin and @yokoonobot. He's also
putting on Fesshole Live shows, which are
huge amount of fun, and you can get news
about tickets from the Twitter account –
but really, do come, the audience
confessions part can often be extraordinary.

When he's not running comedy internet
projects, Rob can be found sleeping,
dicking around with music or attempting to
befriend the crows in Cherry Tree Wood.